branding@thedigitalage

branding@thedigitalage

Edited by

**Herbert Meyers and
Richard Gerstman**

palgrave

First published 2001 by
PALGRAVE
Houndmills, Basingstoke, Hampshire RG21 6XS and
175 Fifth Avenue, New York, N.Y. 10010
Companies and representatives throughout the world

PALGRAVE is the new global academic imprint of
St. Martin's Press LLC Scholarly and Reference Division and Palgrave
Publishers Ltd (formerly Macmillan Press Ltd).

ISBN 0–333–94769–X hardcover

This book is printed on paper suitable for recycling and
made from fully managed and sustained forest sources.

A catalogue record for this book is available
from the British Library.

Library of Congress Cataloging-in-Publication Data has been applied for.

Editing and origination by
Aardvark Editorial, Mendham, Suffolk

10   9   8   7   6   5   4   3   2
10 09 08 07 06 05 04 03 02 01

Printed in Spain by
Mateu Cromo Artes Graficas SA

branding@thedigitalage

contents

Herbert Meyers, Founding Partner
Interbrand Gerstman+Meyers
Richard Gerstman, Chairman
Interbrand US

Bojana Fazarinc, Formerly Director of Global Marketing Services
and Brand Management
Hewlett-Packard Company
From the 30-ton Eniac to the PC ■ Turning raw analog data into
workable information ■ The Internet as an important part of business
■ Using the Internet as a content repository ■ Dividing business
into smaller marketing niches ■ The need for consistency in branding
on the Internet

David B. Green, Senior Vice President of Marketing, Senior
Marketing Officer
McDonald's International
Retailing online and offline ■ Selling the personality of an e-tail brand
■ Marketing e-tailing strategy relevance ■ Building customer

about **the editors**

Richard Gerstman is Chairman of Interbrand US, one of the world's leading brand consultancies. He formed Gerstman+Meyers with designer partner Herbert Meyers in New York City in 1970. In 1996, Gerstman+Meyers became part of the Interbrand Group. The global firm specializes in brand identity, structural and graphic package design, brand strategy and consumer research, and currently serves international corporate clients, including Johnson & Johnson, Kellogg's, AT&T, General Motors and Procter & Gamble. The award-winning firm is a charter member of the Association of Professional Design Firms.

Richard Gerstman has himself won numerous design awards and holds several design and utility patents. He is a member of the Brand Design Association, and a frequent lecturer on marketing and packaging issues.

Herbert Meyers is the retired Founding Partner of Gerstman+Meyers. Born in Germany, he served as an interpreter in the US Army Air Corps in Europe during World War II. On his return to the US, Meyers studied design and has a BA in Fine Arts from Pratt Institute.

After several years of experience as corporate Art Director and design agency Account Manager, Herbert Meyers and Richard Gerstman, in 1970, founded Gerstman+Meyers, a leading brand identity and design consultancy, servicing over a hundred "Fortune 500" clients worldwide.

A past President of Package Design Council International and recipient of numerous design awards, Meyers was the first ever to receive the organization's PDC Award for Lifetime Packaging Excellence and Leadership. He is a member of several professional organizations, including the Pan-European Brand Design Association (PDA).

A frequent lecturer, Meyers co-authored the book *The Marketer's Guide to Successful Package Design* and has contributed chapters to several other professional books.

acknow**ledgments**

In addition to the authors of the twelve chapters in this book and the book's editors, several individuals contributed generously with their time and assistance. In this way, they become active participants in its publication. We gratefully acknowledge their help and encouragement and want to pay tribute to their efforts.

We especially thank two individuals without whose vision this book would not have been born: Tom Blackett, Group Deputy Chairman of Interbrand, who suggested to us the development of a book on the topic of branding and packaging, and Chuck Brymer, Group Chief Executive of Interbrand, without whose enthusiastic support this book would not have been possible.

Perhaps no other visual contribution added as much to the excitement of each of the chapters than the photographic skill of Debby Marcus Brown, a freelance photographer, specializing in custom portraiture and landscape photography. A Commercial Photography and Visual Communications graduate from the University of Delaware, she has spent her career in publishing, media and advertising before joining the Interbrand Group, New York. Debby created all of the portraits of the contributing authors (with the exception of Chapters 6 and 11).

Special commendations belong to Brian Cunningham, a Creative Director at Interbrand's New York headquarters, for art directing the cover graphics and page design of the book. A native of Belfast, Northern Ireland, his love of typography provided a foundation for what has taken him through a wide range of design experiences, from heading up his own design office to his association with several prestigious design groups, prior to joining the Interbrand Group.

Ably assisting Brian in developing the graphics for this book was Interbrand designer Debbie Silva, a recent BFA graduate from the Fashion Institute of Technology in New York City.

Additional tributes belong to Debby Goldberg, Director of Marketing and Public Relations at the Interbrand Group, New York, for some of the editing, and to Carol Belsky for proofreading all of the chapters and other segments of this book. Last but certainly not least, we appreciate the efforts of Maria Tricolla, Executive Assistant at the Interbrand Group, New York, for transcribing our recorded interviews with the chapter authors, correlating the final typescript of this book, and many related tasks.

No efforts in connection with this book should ignore the patience of our beloved spouses for sharing our time and attention with the creation of this book. We believe that they will ultimately participate in our pride in presenting **branding**@the**digital**age to our readers.

herbertmeyers

richardgerstman

Richard Gerstman (left) and Herbert Meyers (right)

intro**duction**

Herbert Meyers and Richard Gerstman

The growth of e-trade during the past few years is, without doubt, the most formidable development in the history of commerce – and there seems to be no foreseeable slowing down. The speed of penetration of this medium into every commercial media is almost incomprehensible to even the most ardent cyber-enthusiasts. Not since the Industrial Revolution of the 19th century has a development so dramatically altered the path of human behavior.

The possibilities of further developments seem literally without limits. Future cyber applications to business, not even explored, seem to have no boundaries. Nor are these developments restricted to interface with current desktop and laptop computers. The increasing appearance of wireless appliances, such as cellular phones, not to mention the infinite means of transmitting and distributing messages from one point to another and the continuing miniaturization of equipment, promise to alter our means of doing commerce throughout the world. Who knows what other, never before invented communication media will surface tomorrow and in the next few years?

The impact this technical revolution is having on retail commerce and on the means we have come to associate with traditional retail marketing is felt more and more every day. It is likely to revolutionize the relationships marketers have with retailers, their channels of distribution, their suppliers, their advertising agencies and their ultimate consumers. Marketers will need to examine how the rocketing cyberspace developments will affect their current and future branding methodologies and determine how and when to adjust them to the ever-growing speed of technological advances.

An article in *Brandweek* recently summed it up as follows: "Today, companies of all sizes are translating their marketing objectives into cyberspace and many are weighing how to replicate their entire marketing effort online."

But will simply *replicating* a current marketing program online be the answer to the e-commerce revolution?

Branding in the 21st century

In looking at the numerous websites that have suddenly surfaced in all categories of commerce, it appears that many of the numerous cyberspace entrepreneurs feel that the Internet is simply another means of communication that requires little, if any, variation from the traditional means of promoting and selling products and services. They have not yet grasped the tremendous potential of promoting their products and services on the Internet to a carefully targeted audience, vis-à-vis the mass communication approach of other media, such as television, that conveys messages to a broad audience in the hope of reaching the few who may be interested in them.

"Traditional Marketing is not dying – it's dead," says Sergio Zyman, a former Chief Marketing Officer of the Coca-Cola Company, in his book *The End of Marketing As We Know It*. "Mass Marketing has lost the ability to move the masses," he continues, "Technology has given people many more options than they had in the past and created a consumer democracy ... Marketers increasingly need to find ways to speak to customers individually, or in smaller and smaller groups."

If this is true, the Internet seems to offer the perfect solution. Marketers are able to communicate with their customers in ways never before possible. The opportunities of interfacing with individuals and smaller, carefully targeted interest groups, and the ability to reach them whenever and wherever they may be at any given moment, are unlimited. Marketers are exploring all this with a variety of approaches, making the Internet a flexible and ever-changing medium. Even marketers, whose products cannot be obtained directly via the Internet, such as fast-food restaurants, use the Internet to communicate a favorable personality and the value of their services to create goodwill among their customers.

In the midst of all this, brand presence emerges as an important means of continuity and interfacing with other communication media. If not, new brands and brandmarks, that surface almost daily on the Internet, can become extinct even before being recognized and accepted by the consumer. The time span for creating new brands and brandmarks has been shortened substantially through the availability of computers and a wide variety of computer software. Many creators of these brands and brandmarks, by being enamored with technology, are ignoring the fact that technology changes so quickly that brands which have not been developed and maintained with thoughtfulness, foresight and in context with their target audience will disappear as quickly as they are born. Thus, the blessings of technology can, if used frivolously, become their creators' demise.

In trying to find answers to how brands can take advantage of this mercurial, not yet fully explored cyber environment, the entrepreneurial spirit of e-commerce marketers is stretched to the limit. As in any revolutionary development, there are pros and cons, ups and downs, and frequently wild fluctuations in productive results. Thus, it comes as no surprise that the e-commerce revolution is going through the same contortions. The enthusiasm and excitement of participating in new and promising ventures that led many investors to overextend their investment contributions in untried and largely inexperienced e-businesses has resulted in many disappointments as ventures faltered and occasionally collapsed under the burden of financial responsibilities. Nevertheless, the electronic means of doing business represents a viable and growing means of commercial enterprise that will unquestionably survive its initial roller coaster course.

Marketers who will surface as leaders in the e-commerce environment will be those who have the wisdom and courage to dimensionalize their branding by combining online and offline communication media. In doing so, they are likely to shape much of our lifestyles in future years. With this in mind, we went to some of these visionaries to let them tell us how they anticipate e-commerce and e-branding to function in the years ahead.

About the book *branding@thedigitalage*

In seeking answers to the still fairly experimental e-commerce experience, we noticed that all of the contributing chapter authors agreed on one issue: that branding will take center stage in e-tailing. But their philosophies and methodologies vary greatly. The diversity of communication methodologies and the variety of visual presentation opportunities available on the web amplify the importance of exploring relevant alternatives to creating and maintaining brands. The lack of control that marketers have over their brands, when promoting their brand through portals such as Yahoo! and AOL, makes the effectiveness of brands on the monitor screen a critical issue. Most noticeably, while control over the placement of brands and packages on brick-and-mortar store shelves has always been of major concern to retailers, the lack of control in the cyberspace world becomes a major concern for brand marketers.

In viewing the current e-commerce websites, one becomes aware of the diversity of emphasis, positioning and overall visual effects of brands on the web. Brands and products often appear in diminutive sizes so that the opportunities for manufacturers and marketers to promote their brands become negligible. In contrast to brick-and-mortar outlets where products are neatly lined up to be viewed and examined at will, dot.com shopping malls consist, more often than not, of alphabetical lists of products, lacking the appeal of packages or other display methods in real-time retailing. To create and maintain branding for the dual requirement of communicating equally well on the web as in the traditional retail environment demands more holistic concepts and makes for difficult choices.

These and other issues will be examined in the chapters of this book as will the authors' views of the online potential of brands to:

- build communities of consumers who can gather and discuss information about brands

- give consumers control of pricing and purchasing as never before

- become global, without the need for international shops and offices

- save advertising costs, through being able to target specific audiences

- gather valuable consumer information through online research

- provide the most effective combination of online and offline marketing

- develop brands and brand strategies specifically for online business

- protect against the online misuse of trademarks and brand names

By taking a brand-focused approach of discussing problems and opportunities encountered by e-marketers in the retail and service industries, the reader will benefit from the 12 visions of business leaders who candidly discuss their views and approaches to e-tailing and e-branding in the new millennium.

bojanafazarinc

Bojana Fazarinc
Formerly Director of Global Marketing Services
and Brand Management

hewlett-packard company

Bojana Fazarinc was until recently the Director of Global Marketing Services and Brand Management at Hewlett-Packard Company, a position she held for five years. In that role, she has had direct responsibility for HP's brand and website strategy development and implementation. In addition, she managed a number of other corporate marketing programs, resulting in a more consistent customer experience across the company.

An HP veteran of over 20 years, Fazarinc has also managed HP's corporate marketing communications function and held a number of other management and marketing positions in HP's rapid business expansion including computing, chemical analysis, medical and test ad measurement. Fazarinc now runs a consulting practice on brand and customer experience management.

1 the internet **explosion**

Like a real physical explosion, the Internet explosion in the past decade not only riveted the attention of the world, but also created sufficient dust, smoke and chaos to limit our ability to see what is happening, where to go or how to survive. As some of the dust and smoke have settled, we are just beginning to realize what has dramatically changed and what is still standing, strong as ever.

This is certainly the case with the topic of branding. Established on a foundation of almost timeless principles, branding in the 1990s was thrown into the complex, confusing Internet context that proclaimed that everything has changed completely and the concept of branding must also be rethought. The extreme hype that has been pervasive in the early Internet years demanded the full revolution of all fundamental business and economic practices, along with their supporting functions, infrastructures and strategies. Today we know that, while the Internet has profoundly changed the world, this transformation, for many things, continues to find its roots in traditional principles and practices. This is certainly true for branding. Instead of a branding revolution, the Internet has created a stimulating rapid evolution of branding's basic concepts, strengthening and expanding their relevance to business and customers. This concept still has at its center the brand promise for an expected customer experience. Against the backdrop of the Internet's technical and business complexity, brand management today is still about understanding what people think and feel, and what motivates them to buy, use and repurchase products, services or ideas. Today, what has changed is that the brand promise has many more possible moments of truth and means of shaping them than ever before. It also means that the brand promise must be more intricately interwoven with business strategy and all its supporting functions.

"Many of the timeless principles of branding do not change. What has changed is an extended dimension of communication vehicles and avenues, an extended dimension of distribution and company or customer contact capabilities."

So, how did this incredible Internet explosion come about and how has branding evolved with it? We must go back farther than the coming of the Internet to understand the catalyst, the key ingredient for its explosion. This key ingredient is, of course, the computer and microprocessor. In the 1940s, the computer referred to a category of people who calculated canon trajectory tables. In its later hardware/software form the computer has given increasingly larger numbers of often less technically oriented users access to the power and capability of changing nearly every facet of our lives.

The first major computer was called the Eniac. In 1946, it was a 30-ton, 1,800 square foot behemoth designed to improve the aim of artillery guns and was operated by highly technical experts. In the following decades, IBM's mainframes expanded from the initial military, governmental application of computers to become a ubiquitous presence in corporate America. Other major computer providers, Control Data, Unysis and such, contributed in further extending computer access to ever larger numbers of corporate technical specialists and university students.

In the 1960s, Hewlett-Packard (HP) further extended computing access to a broad engineering market across a wide range of industries. Primarily a measurement company then, HP invented the 9800 series desktop "calculator" to automate some functions of their measurement instrumentation and turn raw analog data into more workable information. That product could really be considered the first PC, although HP, in its humble way, was reluctant to call it a computer since people's idea of a computer then was an enormous room-size product.

During the 1970s, HP also invented another product that brought computing power into the hands of consumers. That product was the HP-35 handheld calculator. Much more complex and powerful than Texas Instruments' 4-function desk calculators, the HP-35 was initially targeted at engineers and essentially eliminated the slide rule. Its pocket-size appeal, however, rapidly extended to a broader professional and student audience. Within a few years, it was followed by the HP-65 programmable calculator and a calculator wrist watch. With interest in the market growing, many players such as Texas Instruments moved into the marketplace providing huge volume, low-cost computing basics embraced by consumers.

During this same period, great strides were being made in the design of microprocessors that powered these computers. In fact, the symbiosis of computing and microelectronics design became entrenched. In the 1970s, Intel became the most prominent player with its development of the microchip. Their microprocessors made the desktop PC explosion possible and once again stretched computing access to all walks of life, an awesome transition from the 30-ton Eniac in a relatively short period of time.

Major milestones arrived in the 1980s making personal computing pervasive. This included the Apple along with IBM's MS DOS PCs. The IBM PC could be described as a text-oriented operating system. But Apple's Macintosh, with its graphic icons, mouse capabilities and the later advent of Windows by Microsoft, made the whole user interface more appealing and functionally usable for a mass consumer environment. By the early 1990s, perhaps 35% of households in the US owned PCs and it has been growing tremendously worldwide since then.

The huge installed base of PCs in the early 1990s was an essential prereq- uisite to the rapid relevance and acceptance of the Internet. In the late 1970s, the Internet, like the Eniac, started initially as a resource for government agencies and universities. In the following decade, a visionary team of specialists continued to develop the idea of global networking and the novel way of working collaboratively. By the early 1990s, pre Netscape, Mark Andreesen and his team developed Mosaic, the Internet browser and forerunner of Netscape. Mosaic probably had the same impetus for the advancement of the Internet as the iconic interfaces had in the advancement of PCs. Mosaic created the possibility for access to the general marketplace. This was a pivotal time. With a mixture of awe, excitement, inspiration and fear of entering an unknown realm, many companies began to struggle with how to participate in the promise of the Internet.

I remember that I was running the corporate marketing communications function at HP during that time. We had been looking at the concept of electronic sales promotion. We wanted to see how traditional marketing communications activities could move into electronic communication vehicles and repositories. We launched HP's web program as part of the marketing communications function and began the roller coaster ride of exhilaration and exasperation as the complexity and depth of Internet possibilities and demands emerged.

Soon after, the Netscape browser became widely available and there was discussion about Netscape as an alternative operating system for the PC which would be contained within the Internet network. I believe this is what concerned Bill Gates and Microsoft, since their core capability was the operating system which they were not ready to cede. At that point, they started bundling the Microsoft Explorer browser into their operating system which was one of the things that contributed to their legal problems in recent years.

But this bundling of the browser did bring access of these applications to practically everyone buying PCs, for which Microsoft Windows was the predominant operating system. So, I believe that this was another pivotal time for the Internet evolution, in bringing its appeal and acceptance to the general masses.

Parallel to all this was the development of search engines. Although not the first, Yahoo! became the most visible player to realize that in this network it was initially impossible to find things, without specific web addresses to gain information. The concept of being able to search for practically anything using less precise keywords with context was certainly a major development. Although Yahoo!, Alta Vista and other search engine competitors offered this concept, Yahoo! must be credited as a heavily market-oriented e-company. It became necessary for e-brands to now enter the field in a prominent, visible manner and Yahoo! set the stage for these born-on-the-Net companies who also used the traditional media to gain huge market awareness in a short period of time.

Many of the technology companies at that point, including Hewlett-Packard, were realizing that the Internet was becoming a major development, and wanted to be sure to be seen as leaders in the field. Websites started popping up left and right and, at many of these companies, the attitude was to do something fast! Get a domain name – just get something out there – and don't worry about a particular strategy. So initially, I believe companies were using the Net as a content repository. And, in many cases, they were using the Net just as a direct translation of their brochures, data sheets and promotional materials. None of this was organized for easy navigation, nor was it particularly suited for reading on a screen, nor consistent across different parts of the corporation. This initial onslaught of throwing pre-existing content on the Internet, coding it to HTML, and letting customers try to sort through it all was not a compelling way for customers to appreciate the company and the brand.

Adding to that nightmare customer experience, many companies also started loading their websites with snazzy graphics and capabilities which took forever to download. This was the early type of technical showing off, or "technoego," and not a particularly useful or efficient way to give customers the information leading to purchases or brand loyalty.

Despite some blindness about what customers needed from a website experience, companies soon started realizing the power of their websites as a communications/marketing vehicle and distribution channel for researching customers. Some companies, such as Dell, seized the opportunity in an exciting and prominent way, taking their direct marketing model and applying it to the Internet with tremendous success. Dell was essentially set up for delivering through their own distribution, whereas other companies going through resellers and other channels were not in a position to easily transform their business model onto the Net. HP was typical of the companies that struggled with this, since we had a tremendous loyalty to our distribution channel. There was serious reluctance to abandon or create conflict with existing sales channels. Although customers would come to our website, they would leave to buy other computing systems' brands since they were forced to go to dealers to buy PCs. Obviously, customers want one-stop shopping rather than piecing a system together from various distribution points. Dell's web approach put pressure on a number of companies to rethink their distribution and channel strategies. Dell became a great example of a brand which was successful in the direct marketing economy, yet quickly and expertly transitioned to the Internet.

During this time, increasing numbers of companies in the traditional brick-and-mortar space established their websites, and started advertising and trying to brand them within their traditional advertising/communication vehicles. Companies such as Hewlett-Packard would hand out cards at trade shows, send mailers and advertise to try to get people to go to their websites. It worked! In fact, the traffic and growth of the Internet became so tremendous that many companies had difficulty keeping up with their web infrastructure demands and were unable to deliver a very satisfying customer experience. We realized early on that in the past the brand and customer experience were scattered in time and space. Your points of contact, such as a salesperson or brochures, were disparately connected to your advertising and trade shows, so the consistencies of messages were not as obvious.

However, on the Internet, you could move rapidly from awareness of a particular product, or service, to evaluating pricing, purchasing, and actual support within a matter of minutes. Suddenly, in the whole context of this side-by-side concentrated brand experience, inconsistencies of messages and information became blatantly obvious. Decentralized companies at that time faced the challenge of making their marketing communications activities, sales activities and support activities much more integrated and consistent. Yet, getting a consistent message and consistent experience defined across all those different points of the selling/buying cycle and function was nearly impossible for companies that had operated with product fragmented marketing, sales and support activities.

This situation contributed during the 1990s to branding becoming much more prominent, a concept not previously well understood by technology companies. Branding was already an important and prominent capability of consumer companies who understood and better managed the concept of a consistent brand promise and experience. For technology companies in the 1970s and 80s, the product and the technology tended to be the king. It was believed that if you had the superior product or technology, the strategy of, and investment in, branding and marketing was less critical.

But, in the 1990s, that technological differentiation and advantage was becoming more difficult to sustain. Many of these companies were using the same microprocessors, suppliers, and off-the-shelf components which narrowed their product and price differential, creating the need for branding and differentiating through less tangible dimensions.

But branding also started to emerge as an important concern for the technical companies, partly through the experience of the Internet. If the company's website was difficult to navigate, customers would question if the company knew what it was doing – in supposedly its own area of expertise. And, for the first time, this brought home to the traditional technology companies the importance of consistency within their customer or brand experience. What is said and what is promised needed to be delivered. Essentially, on their website, companies needed to demonstrate their under-standing of customer needs. Some born-on-the-Net companies became proficient at managing their brand, but faltered on the profitability of delivering their brand experience.

We started getting a lot more support within my company for a unified approach to our website, which previously had been fragmented by tolerance toward different businesses and product lines wanting to do their own creative thing or doing whatever they felt "their" particular customers needed. Every product line thought it had its own set of customers. But we discovered through Internet research that customers were interested in multiple products that crossed our organizational structure. We were able to track this in an efficient way and find out why customers were coming to our website. These customers navigated across the website and expected an integrated, consistent and unified capability. Customers did not want to separately register for the PC, separately for the printer, separately for the supplies and so forth. What had worked better in the traditional selling and buying process was not well tolerated on the Internet where unified process was expected. This was definitely a time that demanded a consistent way of operating and presenting ourselves to customers across the various states of the buying and selling cycle. This meant that all the different functions and disciplines within the company needed to work in an orchestrated way to deliver a consistent message, because it is very easy for customers to abandon your website and go elsewhere.

Most of the technology companies struggled with similar problems and a desire to build customer confidence in this new communication vehicle and commerce channel. Many large, established companies and new Internet companies joined together to address these common issues in industry associations and consortiums. We worked with IBM, GE, Kodak, AT&T, US West, Microsoft, Sony, and a number of other companies, while I was chairing the board of The Better Business Bureau Online, to establish a reliability and privacy seal program to reassure customers to confidently embrace e-commerce. As we shared our challenges, there was strong agreement that more central, unified management of website marketing, selling and support activities was key not only to strengthening brand and customer experiences, but also in reducing the threat of government regulation and the escalating costs of managing incremental Internet programs. In fact, at Hewlett-Packard, we said our website appeared more like an organization chart than a website that a customer would find useful. Some companies, such as Sony, were so frustrated with their initial website effort that, rather than trying to refine it, they basically started an additional website. Others centralized even more than before.

Cisco was an example of a company that had made great strides in using the Internet as an important part of its business and leveraging it for operating as well as commerce efficiencies. We were learning from our competitors and from other non-competitive companies about Internet issues which were common. It was inevitable that brands and companies had a legacy to overcome, in order to make the Internet work effectively for them.

At the same time, there were companies who were born on the Net and had none of the infrastructure or legacy to overcome or adapt to the Net. Companies such as Amazon.com were able to begin their business models and establish a very prominent brand on the Net. America Online gave people access to the Internet along with providing content. AOL became practically a sub-universe on the Internet. A few years ago, you couldn't open a newspaper or a magazine that didn't have an AOL disk fall out, giving you free hours on AOL. It was a pervasive mass marketing effort in the traditional media to get people onto the Internet and build its brand.

The media, at the same time, added dramatically to the Internet fever. As it promoted the importance of the Internet for the future, people began to feel that if they didn't get their kids on the Internet, the kids would not succeed in school. The frenzy accelerated as tons of money was poured in by venture capitalists to grow new Internet businesses. Internet gurus forecast major changing paradigms that would come and displace established industries and players. Telephone and communication companies realized that chat rooms and other things that people were doing on the Internet enabled them to interface globally without going through standard telephone fees, creating a threat to their existing business models. Then, in addition to the opportunities, the threat of the Internet and its new ways became evident to many traditional corporations that started feeling the need to get involved.

So began the orgy of mergers and acquisitions to plot the gold path to the new market opportunity. Nobody knew who was going to prevail, so you had your traditional companies inserting themselves and buying or merging with new online players in order to stake their claim in the promises of the new economy. The result has been the most crowded and confusing marketplace the world has known.

As companies morphed to new extended businesses, it drove their need to reposition themselves to customers, investors and employees. Branding identity reinventions grew and continue to grow.

While established companies and brands jockeyed for prominence in the online world, new dot.com companies rushed to build brand awareness in traditional ways. Many dot.coms spent more than half their venture financing on brand development. E*TRADE, for example, spent close to $300 million in 1999 on advertising. While this unprecedented spending to build new brands was successful for some online businesses such as Amazon.com and AOL, other dot.coms failed to establish a customer relevance with enough scale and revenue to sustain ongoing brand-building efforts. It has always been said that nothing kills a brand faster than creating broad-based awareness and expectation through advertising before a company has developed an appealing, relevant and fully functional customer experience. Nowhere is this saying more true than online, where concentrated, side-by-side customer experiences – across all stages of the selling/buying cycle – create more opportunities to weaken the brand. Customers go to the Internet to save time and increase convenience. Any experience that obstructs a hassle-free experience, from slow response times, confusing navigation, unresponsive service or inadequate information, undermines brand equity and loyalty. This, in turn, demands tight integration and consistency across all marketing, sales, support and service strategies and tactics that shape a consistent, compelling customer experience.

The Internet enabled and accelerated another evolution for branding. The brand experience that once spanned the period between a customer's awareness and purchase of a product is now increasingly the beginning of an ongoing relationship, a relationship that includes an array of after-market loyalty services that include but overshadow the physical product. While loyalty programs existed before the Net, the Net has opened up enormously expanded, more affordable and strategically creative ways to do loyalty programs. For years United Airlines had their Mileage Plus, a very successful loyalty program. But companies such as Kodak and HP launched or expanded into website loyalty programs and web communities of people with similar interests, where a customer could learn how to get the most from the product or services purchased. The goal of these programs is to have customers constantly expand their ability to benefit from the purchase and the relationship with the company. Such programs also gave companies the ability to sell additional products and services.

At the same time, some really core traditional aspects of branding have not changed at all. A brand is still a promise. It is a predictable set of capabilities or experiences that a customer can count on from a company, product or service. It still requires both consistency and differentiation. So many of those timeless principles of branding do not change. What has changed is an extended dimension of communication vehicles and avenues, an extended dimension of distribution and company or customer contact capabilities. What the Internet has done is to expand the ways a customer can come into contact with the brand. It has put added pressure on companies and brands to make sure that across all points of contact, across all moments of truth, the consistency and the branded experience is brought forth in a unified and predictable way, a way that really delivers on the brand promise. While established consumer companies with established brands already practice this, the larger technology companies still have a lot of challenges in accomplishing this complex orchestration.

Contributing to effective loyalty programs has been the ability of the online environment to track and measure more quantitatively and qualitatively a customer's online interaction. That, along with the ability to target and customize online marketing/messaging programs, has dramatically helped to advance customer relationships management (CRM) online and offline. All in all, the Net has set an amazing foundation for managing and enhancing the total customer and brand experience for a company and its various customer segments.

In the dawn of the new millennium, companies large and small are increasingly grasping the ever-expanding potential of the Internet and how to leverage it for their business goals. Still, the many creative, innovative business and marketing strategies that have emerged have not been able to fully tap the incredible technological capabilities of the Net. It's no wonder. Besides the daily developments of new products and solutions to improve the Net as a powerful communications vehicle and sales channel, there is a major wireless capability taking shape. A capability that will once again challenge businesses to find creative new ways to connect with customers, further expanding the points of contact in a customer or brand experience.

Against this backdrop of complexity of technology and business strategies is the ongoing pressure by consumers to make Internet interactions with companies simpler and more intuitive. On the other hand, companies have embraced the Internet for the promise of cost efficiencies in managing their customer interaction. Some of the initial ideas of how to accomplish this may need to evolve if positive brand images and customer satisfaction are to be maintained. For example, most companies have tried to gain sales efficiencies by cutting out the salesperson and leaving the customers on their own to navigate through websites to make a purchase. The result has been that 65% of the sales transactions across all industries that are initiated online are abandoned. They're abandoned because generally, at the last moment, there may be a question or something in terms of the navigation that has not been appropriately designed or executed to make it easy for the customer to get that last-minute reassurance to close the sale. If companies really want their customers to complete the transaction and not go to another website, they may need to inject a type of human interface. Some companies currently have "help" buttons or audio connections to help the consumer. In the future, there may be low-cost ways to address this problem in a more compelling manner. Websites will have the ability to represent a call center operator in a visual way, perhaps through a branded character, that will be more compelling and bring some of the emotional connection which often closes the sale. If you go into a retail store, initially you may not want to be bothered while you're evaluating things. But, when you get down to the final purchase, it's nice to have a salesperson there to confirm some last-minute information. Online, video won't be a viable option for some years since it consumes a huge amount of bandwidth. However, through Avatar's low bandwidth, consuming graphic representations of an actual call center operator, a website can have facial and hand expressions captured and transmitted that could be a realistic representation of a person or it could be a branded character. So, soon, if a customer presses the help button, she may get live interaction with a call center operator graphically represented as a Pillsbury Doughboy or other branded character. The sale can be closed by this branded interface, which has a personal and more emotional context at that critical moment of sale. In the wireless mode, instead of scrolling through screens, an avatar, or branded character, could guide you and talk to you through audio, reinforcing some dimension of the image that brands want to create with their customers.

The whole concept of managing a customer experience will continue to be of major importance and greater complexity particularly as the Net makes possible more and more sequential branding. In some ways, the Internet is bringing the world closer, but, in other ways, it is also permitting us to begin to divide into smaller tribes and market niches. Each of these niches will be treated in ways that are consistent with their needs, interest and a particular kind of customer experience. In the future, the companies and brands will have to dig much deeper in terms of gaining customer insight, strategically defining their customer segments, and defining the type of experiences that each of those customers will need in order to build brand loyalty and a competitive advantage. As before, companies and brands will need to define the critical moments of truth and the contact points for each of those experiences, and manage those experiences much more expertly across the disciplines and functions of the company. This includes e-selling, e-marketing, e-support, and e-loyalty-building programs. More than ever, the successful brand will be embedded in every aspect of a company's business design and organizational system. Across that entire spectrum, the comprehensive definition of these customer or brand experiences will help to shape and guide the way companies manage their brands and achieve competitive advantage.

davidgreen

David B. Green
Senior Vice President of Marketing
Senior Marketing Officer
mcdonald'sinternational

David B. Green is Senior Vice President of Marketing for McDonald's Corporation and Senior Marketing Officer, McDonald's International. In his role, he is responsible for the direction and overall supervision of McDonald's marketing activities around the world. Before assuming these responsibilities in 1996, he was directly responsible for developing and overseeing all marketing activities for McDonald's in the US. He joined McDonald's in 1972 and has held successive management positions in McDonald's Field and National Marketing Departments. He was promoted to Vice President of National Marketing in 1985, and in 1990 was appointed Senior Vice President of Marketing.

2 from retailing **to e-tailing**

A strong brand is a strong brand wherever you experience it. The basic elements of branding are the same whether they are applied to the retail environment, in-store merchandising, e-commerce, or websites. Branding still relies totally on the customer's experience. The art of branding today, in this time of high technology, is no different than it has been over the past hundred years. The principals are the same. Only the pace and complexity of options have increased geometrically, dramatically increasing the speed of success or failure. In the end, brands that understand themselves and their customers the best, and then consistently execute against that focused understanding, have the best chance of long-term profitable success.

Of course, the channels through which the brand is conveyed are important because they help you to reach your target audience, indicate whether you're modern or contemporary, and help to sort out your prime prospects.

Yet the basic attribute of a strong brand is consistent throughout all
channels. Branding is essentially a universal marketing force working
constantly to influence the consumer.

McDonald's went through an interesting process a couple of years ago.
We're a retailer with a 45-year history, 28,000 restaurants and 43 million
customers a day. And as a retailer, we have to touch each and every one of
those customers. In fact, McDonald's has an "audience" as large as most
US networks such as ABC, CBS or NBC, so nobody touches people like
McDonald's does, throughout 120 countries.

With all this history, we certainly knew what our brand represented, but we
never sat down with our own top management to systematically define the
essence of both the McDonald's brand and the McDonald's experience. So,
in early 1999, we went through a process with a diverse group of our top
executives from around the world, including extensive benchmarking of our
customers and other companies, to decide how we wanted to define the
McDonald's brand. What does McDonald's stand for, what has it stood for
through our 45-year history and what is the *promise* of the brand? This
included defining our personality, the values we share with our customers
and the rewards and benefits they receive from coming to our restaurants.
What features should the McDonald's brand stress consistently throughout
the world in all our locations? And, how do we make sure we are relevant in
every community and channel of communication where we do business?

The answers that came out of this process didn't surprise anyone. But the
journey we took to get there was a terrific way to align and focus a very
large and decentralized company. And what did we find? First and
foremost, McDonald's is fun. We are a fun experience. People enjoy coming
to us. We can't take ourselves too seriously. We serve delicious handheld
sandwiches and fries, but it's the personality of the experience of eating that
food that's most important.

What is the manifestation of this experience? It's the expectation that we will try to make you, the customer, feel special and always put a smile on your face. In fact, I'd say the whole mission of McDonald's is to try to make you feel special and to make you smile. We captured it in the following statement: "With a sense of fun and youthful spirit, we will proudly serve an exceptional McDonald's eating experience that makes all people feel special and makes them smile – every customer, every time." This is not an advertising slogan. It's the McDonald promise; a promise of shared values, fun and youthful spirit. That's our brand.

We further defined the brand through nine key attributes that we felt demonstrated the essence of McDonald's. We need to be the most affordable, the best food of its type, the cleanest and safest, no matter where you are, on a consistent basis. We're always welcoming and inviting, no matter who you are, whether you're rich or poor. We're the fastest and easiest to use. With all the locations we have, we're the most convenient. We're committed to the community. Our special relationship is not just global, it's local. We truly care for kids and try to personalize the visit and personalize the experience through choice and variety.

We also realized that key icons represent the McDonald's brand to our customers, icons such as the Golden Arches, the big, red fry box, Ronald McDonald, and even the mansard roof and roof beams. When our customers see them, they immediately establish the expectation of a McDonald's visit.

And most important, to make all of this work, are our people, the more than 1.5 million employees around the world that ensure that the McDonald's experience is delivered to each customer, one at a time. Our people have a commitment of pride and enthusiasm, and, as a brand, we need to promise our employees nothing less than we promise our customers.

We documented our brand platform through what we call the McDonald's Pyramid, and sent it out to every employee, because we wanted everybody throughout the world to understand it. It becomes, in a sense, a universal pair of glasses to look through and a way to judge whether the things you're doing today and for tomorrow are on track in enhancing our brand.

> *"Whether you experience McDonald's through our restaurants, our website or e-commerce, the values and personality of our brand must shape that experience."*

Whether you experience McDonald's through our restaurants, our website, or e-commerce, these are the values and personality of our brand that must shape that experience. We realize that a company like McDonald's does not really have goods or services that can be easily sold over the Internet. We're not going to sell our hamburgers in cyberspace anytime soon. So, what can we sell over the Net? We're selling our personality and selling the fact that our brand means a lot more than hamburgers or french fries. And, this personality and experience has to come through, whether you're watching a TV commercial, reading a billboard, sitting in our restaurant, or visiting our website. So, that's the backbone of how we started looking at how to put our e-tailing strategy together. We had to interface with our consumers with the same kind of personality that we have in our restaurants and the same values you see in our advertising and marketing. So, if you go into McDonald's.com, it's going to be fun, there will be a sense of youthful spirit, and community. You can go in there as a child, have fun with Ronald McDonald and play games. You can go there as a mom and find interesting activities and things to do with your children. You can go there as a prospective employee and find out all about the opportunities. And you can go there as an investor and find out information about McDonald's from an investment point of view, but all within the context of our brand personality.

We also want our consumers to know that we are very much a local, community-specific, culturally relevant company in every country that we serve. So, you can surf the world through our website, for example, and go to Japan and see what life is like McDonald's-wise in Japan. You can go to France and see what McDonald's is like on the Champs-Elysées. You can go to Latin America, to Asia/Pacific, to the Middle East, and visit these different countries and cultures in order to feel this kind of cultural relevance that McDonald's has throughout the world. This is very important for us.

One of the key success factors for McDonald's is the ability to take our basic brand strategy and then make it culturally relevant for each of the communities and countries we serve in the world. If you visit another country, you might find different nuances in our menu, in our restaurant experience, in the iconography that we use and the restaurant positioning, but the values and experience should be the same. We try to position McDonald's like a good friend, a friend that might dress a little differently depending on the occasion, but has the same personality no matter where we are in the world. That personality needs to be just as consistent online.

We're cognizant that McDonald's is a retail location driven by dedicated owner operators and local partners around the world. So, we need to make sure that what we do on the Internet for our brand influences customers to come into our restaurants, and reinforces their in-restaurant experience. This is a time of significant experimentation. I believe most brick-and-mortar retailers don't yet have successful (profitable) strategies to sell their goods or services through the Internet. So many retailers are going through the same process. We understand how to get our personality on the Internet, and know we have to provide value within the context of that personality, but we still have to figure out ways to deliver that personality in a more retail manner via the Internet. Experimenting with a number of approaches will give retailers the greatest opportunity for success. For McDonald's, some examples of this web-based consumer activity experimentation are the ability to place large takeout orders over the Net, book birthday parties on the Net, and take a virtual restaurant tour to see how we make our burgers and run our restaurants.

One of the important assets of McDonald's, especially when it comes to experimentation, is our worldwide distribution and decentralization. By having locations in 120 countries, and at the same time striving to make each country self-sufficient, we have the best of both worlds. We have taken our efforts with the Internet and said to every country, "Here's our personality and our consistent brand values. Now, within this context, you go out and experiment and try to find ways to make e-commerce and the Internet come alive for our customers." As a result, we have literally hundreds of hotbeds of Internet activity that we can share and evaluate around the world.

Since convenience plays such an important role for a retailer such as McDonald's, we have already started to use the Internet to capitalize on our many locations. We have a restaurant locator and mapping function so that customers can find their nearest McDonald's. They can even print out a trip map listing all of the McDonald's restaurants along the way on their local or cross-country travels. We're in the process of adding details about each restaurant. Does it have a play place for my child, is there anything special about that particular McDonald's that would be interesting for me? What's the décor? We're continually looking for ideas that connect to the customer through the restaurant, and related ideas for the Internet that give a virtual experience which will eventually make the restaurant visit more valuable. We're combining the best of the Internet with the best of the restaurant experience.

One of the big opportunities for local retailers is to use the Internet as a virtual community meeting place. McDonald's restaurants have been the community meeting place in many parts of the world. We have little league teams come in to celebrate victories and defeats, and many small groups have their coffee klatches at breakfast at McDonald's. This is an area of great potential over the Net. For example, you'd be able to go, virtually, to your local McDonald's and find out what's happening in your community. What's going on at the little league team, the Kawanis Club? You might even find a video of your child at a local community event.

There really isn't any other retailer like McDonald's with 28,000 locations around the world. McDonald's could be its own ISP. We are a trusted friend connected with almost every community, so you could get on the Internet, surf, and do things in the community with McDonald's as a family portal. That's part of the overall philosophy of who we are. The opportunities are unlimited. With a trusted brand, parents can look at us and say, if McDonald's is doing something on the Net, then I know it will be great for my entire family.

Given the McDonald's trusted friend personality, the Internet has the potential to establish closer, more robust relationships with the consumer. We can have a one-on-one relationship with a family or a particular consumer, providing value to them by giving them information, knowledge, entertainment or whatever it might be that fits within the overall context of the brand. Take the Olympics, one of our alliance partners. We form a better relationship with consumers by using the Olympics as a way for them to think about our brand. We do that in our restaurants with promotions and public relations events and on the Internet with live chats and diaries of the athletes, bringing the Olympic Games a little closer into your home. The big challenge to retailers is to take their own personality and brand positioning and add the appropriate alliance partners to this value through the Internet. Since our brand and the Olympic "brand" share so many similar values, this makes the partnership work in the customer's mind. Retailers need to address the kind of content and value that can be added for a stronger relationship online.

One challenge to building customer relations online is the issue of privacy and information collection. I believe that companies such as McDonald's and their customers are going to have to come to some kind of understanding about the kind of data we can collect in order to provide additional value. How much information should customers be willing to give in order to get that additional value? McDonald's is very cautious about this issue, and we don't currently collect personal information on our websites because of all the children who visit. But, as we look down the road and we talk about having clubs or organizations or virtual communities that we want to build, we will need some information about people's interests, in order to be able to provide content and give value. Eventually, retailers will come to an under-standing with their customers about the kind of information that they can collect in order to give value back to them.

When you have 43 million people visiting your outlets every day, you have a lot of e-retailers and portals out there that would just love to have those people as their customers. Selecting the right alliances and partners is very important to enhancing and growing your brand. If the customer sees your partners as *not* adding value, it could have a very detrimental effect on your brand. Lots of start-up companies in Internet commerce come to us and say that they can add value to our customers. Before we start any potential alliance, we have to ask ourselves a number of questions. Are the two brands truly compatible? Do they share the same values? If you were to ask our customers about a potential alliance, would they say, "Wow, that makes sense ... that would be really neat!" Obviously, the brand values have to be compatible across the board since you don't want to confuse your customer. This goes back to some of the basic aspects of branding. You don't own the brand, McDonald's doesn't own our brand – our customers own the brand. Our customers are the only ones who really give a brand power. That's one of the reasons why the Disney relationship has been so good for us. That's because the customer looks at us as they look at Disney and they understand. They say to themselves that there aren't two better companies on earth that have the same kind of values when it comes to families and kids than Disney and McDonald's.

The Internet aside, we only have three very visible global alliances. One of them is the Olympics, where we are a top sponsor. The other is World Cup Soccer – an incredible passion for people around the world. And the third is Disney. By having an insight into people's passions about sports, entertainment, families and dreams, and striving to be the best, we have put together a very compatible group of alliance partners that makes ultimate sense to our customers.

Over the past couple of years, some enormous brands have been built on the Internet alone, such as Yahoo! and Amazon. There are a lot of them out there. But, my sense is that the consumer does not want an incredibly easy interface with a virtual retailer alone. They also want a one-on-one, face-to-face, "high-touch" relationship. Just look at the analogy with our drive-thru's. The typical restaurant drive-thru starts with a speaker box. You talk into a speaker; someone talks back to you. You might get a graphic display of your order. But, you don't make direct contact with a real person. That's why we now have a lot of new restaurants with what we call "face-to-face" drive-thru. You drive up and you're looking face to face at the order taker. You're talking with them and conversing and ordering, and they're taking it down. I believe the human psyche says, "Okay, I can have a kind of anonymous virtual relationship with someone, but I'd still like to have that augmented with a personal relationship." So, from my perspective, I think eventually you're going to see a convergence, where some of the best of the Net and some of the best of the brick-and-mortar world, will come together or work together.

In the future, retailers will be serving their customers who want to use the Internet, but who also want to actually talk to someone and touch and feel the product as well. Retailers are still struggling with the issue, and the Sears, Wal-Marts and Best Buys are trying to figure out the best way to handle it. Undoubtedly, a more personal interface will make its way into the overall e-commerce experience. People who have a problem will find someone to talk to directly (maybe through the Internet), and if they have to return something, they will be able to go to a brick-and-mortar store. Many customers want to have this feeling of personal contact with the retailers they deal with. Some retailers now, even without broadband, are using "chat" technology to talk to their customers. If you have a problem or don't understand something, you just click a button and all of a sudden someone's coming online asking, "Can I help you?"

From both a retail and customer perspective, there is still some resistance to just taking your product, putting it online, and expecting customers to buy it. I see it through my two sons, who are very e-literate. One is 26 and the other 23 and they know exactly what's happening on the Net. They go online, chat, search, have fun. But when it finally comes to buying a significant purchase, they want the touchy, feely experience they get in a store. My son will go on the web for all kinds of information about a new TV, about the manufacturer, about the best prices. But, when it finally comes down to it, he wants to walk in somewhere and look at it, see it and feel it. This is especially true with a major purchase. He might eventually buy it online, but only after he has gone to the retail outlet, found out whether it's something he really likes and whether the brand fits his personality. Then he might go to the Internet and try to find the best deal. But, he is still very reluctant to purchase online because he is unsure of what might happen if something goes wrong. So, there's this combination of the high-touch and the high-tech, and I think retailers in the future will need to work this out to maximize their sales potential.

McDonald's retail strategy will have to be this combination of both offline and online, figuring out how to provide added value to the customer through the Internet while reinforcing the in-restaurant experience. The future for a retailer is not taking an entire retail line and retail experience away from the brick-and-mortar store and putting it online. It's all a matter of degrees. The quantity of "degrees" on the Internet will depend on the retailer. The smart retailers will work with the consumer to say, "How can I take part of the buying experience and put it on the Internet without totally replacing that highly emotional, personal, interactive experience that retailers have in the store?"

Whether talking about the Internet or just plain retailing and brand building, brand loyalty comes from setting expectations and then exceeding them. You set consumer expectations through each channel of communication and then you either meet or exceed those expectations on a very consistent basis. For McDonald's, it is all about making and then delivering on the McDonald's promise. When you experience the brand, it should make you and your family smile. Even though it's an experience that happens often, it still has to be special. Loyalty is not necessarily about promotion, or deals, or price alone – but overall, loyalty is about getting what I expected whenever and wherever I interact with your brand. It's that simple. Meeting and exceeding customer expectations is the whole ball game.

A good perspective for any company trying to exceed customer expectations is to "stick close to their knitting." Understand exactly what you stand for in the customer's mind and the unique benefits and values you need to deliver to your key targets, and then deliver it with incredible, tenacious focus and clarity. And, if you start to waiver too far from your core, I guarantee loyalty will go away. That doesn't mean that a strong brand can't be leveraged or stretched either online or offline. McDonald's has a full line of kids clothing in partnership with Wal-Mart, called "McKids." It's one of the top three brands of children's clothing in the US. The reason McKids is so successful is that it has the same kind of brand attributes our restaurants have – fun, great value, quality and consistency. Our experience with McKids gives us confidence that by leveraging our values and personality, we can provide the same value and success in the world of e-commerce.

While we're very interested in looking at all approaches to e-commerce, we can't let that distract us from delivering the core business in our brick-and-mortar restaurants. We've separated a group of people from the business, and put them in a different location to think about, innovate, and make those quick decisions on how to manage many aspects of e-commerce and e-business. This way, it doesn't distract from the overall base of our business. This group reports directly to the top management team and communicates with a series of boards made up of mid-level management, so their work product can be directly integrated into the organization where appropriate. We're finding this the best way to get up to full speed Net-wise, while keeping momentum everywhere else.

Will McDonald's Internet activities change any of our marketing and advertising activities? Ultimately, they must. We will find ways of addressing specific target audiences in more efficient ways by targeting them through the Internet. We're starting to do that with children, teens, and moms. Certainly, the art of customer relationship management has been redefined by the potential of the Internet and e-commerce. But, leveraging the potential into reality will be greatly influenced by the issues that we have discussed above: branding, high-tech, high-touch, privacy, consistency, expectation setting, alliance management, and so on.

McDonald's has always found a way to remain contemporary and fun, and weave ourself into the lives of our customers. The more channels that we can use to touch them, and the more places they can find a familiar and comfortable McDonald's experience, the more chances we have of developing customer loyalty. The Internet is playing an ever-greater role in our customers' daily lives. McDonald's must appear there – and appear in such a way that we add value to their lives consistent with our brand. Strong brands constantly adapt to changing consumer trends and habits, searching for new ways and new ideas to develop and reinforce customer loyalty, while maintaining a strong consistent brand personality. The rules haven't changed because of the Internet. It's just that the pace has picked up a bit, as we incorporate e-tailing into retailing.

fred**horowitz**

Frederick J. Horowitz
Co-founder

netgrocer.com

Frederick J. Horowitz, now Chairman and CEO of Sumner Capital, LLC, is an active investor in early stage technology and turnaround consumer product companies. Prior to starting Sumner Capital, Horowitz, a founding investor in NetGrocer, joined the management of NetGrocer in November 1998 as President and CEO to implement a new business model aimed at building sales and cutting costs. During the two years of Horowitz's leadership, the new management team initiated strategies that dramatically improved the site for the customer, providing greater ease of use and value. Sales grew substantially over the past two years as the company has positioned itself as the premier e-commerce selling engine for the leading consumer product companies.

3 e-retailing: **a look ahead**

Great merchandising is the key to success for most retailers, online and offline. Great retail brands are not built through advertising, but through store use, through being in front of your customers, and by being at the right place with the right product at the right time.

Most of the failures of e-tailers during the past were caused by brand managers who were brought in to run the e-tailers and confused brand building (great for cookies) with successful merchandising (the core to building a retailer). With the Pets.com sock puppet leading the way, one needs few other examples. Above all, the experiences of the past few years have shown that the traditional rules for successful retailing are no different in the online world than in the traditional brick-and-mortar world.

Despite recent difficulties, this new medium is only five years old and will have an incredible impact on how consumers shop, retailers sell, and manufacturers create their brands. The key to understanding the Internet's impact on retailing lies in comprehending that the Internet is not so much a separate retail channel as it is an extraordinary tool to accelerate and streamline all aspects of a retail business. In fact, the best way to view the Internet is to understand that it is simply an incredible database of knowledge and information that is sortable, approachable, and actionable whenever and wherever you want.

> *"The more things change, the less they change."*
> *– Old French Proverb*

The Internet functions like a lubricant, improving and reducing the friction in an existing machine. Therefore, as different as it feels, it is still a tool to be used for good or bad. The winners will successfully integrate it in order to leverage their existing strengths. The losers will look at it as a separate module from their everyday business.

No matter how powerful the technology, the goal of Internet retailing, like brick-and-mortar retailing, is to aggregate and then distribute manufacturers' products in a manner that provides real value to consumers and manufacturers. If no value is created, either through passing on cost savings of e-business to the consumer, or through a truly improved shopping experience, then the e-retailer will not last longer than the amount of cash it has in the bank. If you want to create a successful e-retail brand, you must create real value through an extraordinarily broad selection of products along with better prices and/or through an incredible information-rich shopping experience built around a narrower product selection. This is the core of good merchandising.

Consumers use products from many different manufacturers, and the need to aggregate as many as possible into each shopping experience is what really justifies nationwide Internet retailing as well as brick-and-mortar retailing and justifies the shipping costs associated with it. The sites that give the most solutions and actionable content, aggregated into one box, with one reasonable shipping cost, will be the winners.

NetGrocer provides a useful window for understanding some of the opportunities and pitfalls of bringing e-commerce to retailing. The founders of NetGrocer.com understood that the key value of NetGrocer was created through using the Internet as a nationwide ordering and marketing tool to offer its customers low-cost "aggregation." The consumer can aggregate a very wide selection of products, including food, health and beauty, pet products, and even hard-to-find products. These are all shipped in one box with one relatively low shipping fee.

On the other hand, traditional grocery retailing's greatest value to consumers is its provision of the world's freshest produce at a very low cost combined with a selection of regional and national brand dry goods located in the "center" of the store. Because we felt we could not improve on their perishable solution, NetGrocer chose to compete as a "category killer" focused on dry perishables shipped nationwide via a three-day service from Federal Express. We don't try to solve the problem of where to buy the "fun stuff" – dairy, meat, fish. We solve the customer problem of getting those "boring" dry perishables which one finds in the center of the grocery store.

These "replenishment"-oriented products are the core of NetGrocer's offering along with those non-perishables that are "hard-to-find." Being a nationally available source of hard-to-find products gives NetGrocer a strong consumer hook and reason for consumer trial and use of the site.

NetGrocer takes the stock staples that people buy week in and week out, and creates an opportunity for repeat purchasing that is easier than the replenishment portion of the traditional shopping experience. NetGrocer reduces duration and frequency of trips to the store. With no store overheads and a lower level of inventory (but not necessarily SKUs), NetGrocer is also able to provide a lower cost transaction, especially on slower moving hard-to-find products.

Consumers are multichannel, with and without the Internet. The most common criticism I hear about NetGrocer is that we are not a "total solution" for the consumer because we do not provide a delivery method for the purchase of perishable products. With over 100 million American households, there is a wide range of demographic groups with very diverse needs. The same consumer may shop at Costco (the global discount chain) on Monday and at Barney's (New York clothier) on Tuesday. Yet on Wednesday, he may visit a CVS.com (the online division of the national US health care and pharmacy chain). Because there is no one solution in the retailing business, consumers will continue to be multiplatformed in terms of retailers. A Kroger store visit on Monday, and a NetGrocer purchase on Tuesday, to send food to their weekend home, is the reality that consumers need multiple solutions from multiple sources to manage their diverse needs. Webvan has gone the way of most retailers who believed they offered a "total solution" to consumers' shopping needs.

Fulfillment is a key to the future in e-retail, and consumer direct fulfillment is an incredible logistics operation that's way outside the standard skill of a traditional grocer. It's a skill that needs to be developed (or more likely acquired) if traditional retailers are going to successfully harness the opportunities of the Internet. Traditional retailers will need to partner with a company such as NetGrocer, which is focused on the center of the store, so that the grocer/partner can focus on the perishable experience. Ahold and its recent purchase of Peapod was a relatively inexpensive way to jump start their home delivery business and to offer their customers a multiple channel shopping option. In addition, they proved the old saying that "the second mouse gets the cheese."

E-commerce linked to fulfillment won't be for all brick-and-mortar retailers, because some stores will offer value to their customers through other means without the link to a fulfillment solution. But, even these brick-and-mortar stores may still use e-business to make their supplier chain dramatically more efficient or to offer better promotions towards driving in-store traffic. An important lesson is that e-tailing, with its link to fulfillment, should not be confused with e-business; using electronic means to improve the infrastructure of a business.

The web is no different than the brick-and-mortar world in the need for the retailer to create value for its suppliers. Wal-Mart may be the lowest *gross* margin account for many manufacturers, but, for most of those same companies, they are the highest *net* margin account because of the efficiency with which they work to jointly create savings with their suppliers.

NetGrocer created, through its electronic couponing service, real value for both the manufacturers and the consumers. The customer doesn't cut the coupon, the manufacturer doesn't print or distribute it, and the retailer doesn't have to pay for redeeming it. This is giving real value through savings, and is one of the revolutionary things that NetGrocer has done to the grocery business that makes us recognized as a strong brand by both consumers and manufacturers. In the future, the coupons will also be portable across all retail channels in the form invented by NetGrocer's coupon partner, OneClip.com.

E-tailers create value in many other ways. For example, an e-tailer can provide manufacturers with the means to offer the consumer discounts based on loyalty over time from the purchase of individual units of product. The consumer won't need to buy six units of a product all at once in order to receive discounts, as they do currently at club stores. With e-tailing, the

consumer buys these products as they need them, and, not unlike accruing frequent flyer miles, is rewarded with loyalty discounts credited directly into their online accounts. The manufacturer won't give the dollars in promotion and trade allowances, but will put the marketing dollars right into the loyal consumer's pocket. This is a new loyalty opportunity, quite different from today's concept of product loyalty, and much more cost efficient for the manufacturer.

Value needs to be real, not just perceived. Many leading brick-and-mortar grocers confused promotional tools such as Priceline.com with developing a real web-based retailing strategy. I believe that the Priceline model was the ultimate in product disloyalty, because the consumer did not bid on a brand, but on a product category. It was a promotional tool similar to a coupon. Consumers were loyal to the Priceline brand, but not loyal at all to the manufacturers' brands. Because Priceline did not provide any value to the manufacturers and was actually destructive to the value of their brands, Priceline was unable to get funds to support its business model from the consumer product companies. Fortunately, this experiment was stopped before the retailers were forced to bid against each other for the consumers' business.

Nationwide e-tailers, with their repeat order systems, shopping list functions, and product loyalty-based savings, are the ultimate brand builder for the consumer product companies. The most profitable opportunity online for the consumer product companies will be to focus on those retailers with whom they can deliver repeat purchases over time through a combination of online and offline loyalty-based promotions.

Today, the consumer product companies have the greatest opportunity they've had in over 20 years to beat back the private (own) label and inefficient trade promotions that, in some cases, have taken control of their brands. The brick-and-mortar supermarkets, through slotting fees and trade allowances, have increased the cost of doing business for the manufacturer, while allowing themselves to provide a private label product at a dramatically lower cost. Our passion to provide value to the consumer drove us to be one of the only American grocers not to demand slotting fees (the legalized bribe that the manufacturer pays the retailer to get their product onto the shelf). NetGrocer's goal was to be merchants, not end-aisle display salesmen.

If you visit Nabisco.com and you click on to buy, you're led to a Nabisco store "powered" by NetGrocer. This is more than just a link. It really is a commerce solution that gives the consumer product company a way to merchandise its own store. Suddenly, through their websites, the consumer product companies are able to make real sales through a co-branded store powered by NetGrocer. They're becoming a retailer through the doorway to our site.

With clever marketing and utilizing the power of the web, products that were non-brands can again become national brands. We did this with Quisp Cereal (www.quisp.com). As an alternative distribution channel, there will be wonderful opportunities on the web to create or rebuild fallen angels, fallen brands. Some products may be slow moving in a thousand brick-and-mortar stores, but in three centralized NetGrocer warehouses they become fast-moving items worth holding onto and manufacturing.

Using its commerce software to provide the "store within a store" solution, NetGrocer has attracted a wide range of consumer product companies as its partners. This is a unique enabling tool for the manufacturers to sell directly to their consumers. Now that the consumer product companies have tasted the fruit of consumer direct, they will find ways to continue investing in supporting their ability to connect directly with consumers.

If you bring this solution to its logical conclusion, one can envision a food service solution that enables direct selling to office managers, small restaurants and even small retail stores. This is what Nestlé and NetGrocer started with Nestléoffice.com.

Nestlé has one of the leading coffee brands and they have a nationwide online office coffee service (www.Nestléoffice.com). That's a solution. They're not selling Nescafé, they're selling Nestlé office coffee service, which has the ability to offer non-Nestlé products because NetGrocer is providing the commerce engine and the fulfillment.

A very important strength of online retailing and presentation of products is the opportunity for "solution selling." Solution centers will bring a whole new approach to e-commerce. E-tailing brings cross-category selling opportunities, not just in grocery, but in sporting goods and everything else. Selling, via solutions, will be one of the most profitable tools that any retailer or manufacturer will have. They'll be able to create custom solutions and be able to really sell to a customer, no matter who the customer is or what demand group the customer is from. For example, if you sell diabetic products and you have a brand that's focused on sugar-free products, you can drive traffic to a diabetic solution store powered by NetGrocer. Whether a diabetic, a new mother, or an athlete, an e-retailer can create that solution store around them. The traditional brick-and-mortar store doesn't have enough shelf space to put all these new items in one place.

Brick-and-mortar stores put the baby products in one place, health care in another, and vitamins for pregnancy in another area. Therefore, everything is split up in the brick-and-mortar store, whereas with online solution retailing, all these items can be bundled together as a "new mother" shelf. Solutions and category depth of products are becoming more important than cross-category width. Solution selling is a powerful tool for manufacturers to use to regain control over their brands and provides the justification for much of the recent industry consolidation.

Merchandising through solution merchandising also takes away the need for impulse selling. Solution-oriented merchandising becomes normal selling. Impulse becomes planned because the products are always on the "correct" shelf. That is the future.

In the future, replenishment-oriented shopping will become a more passive task as replenishment becomes its own solution. Once consumers set up their preferences, retailers, both traditional and only online, will know what consumers like, how they like it and email solutions will arrive. For example, if you like to sail, you'll get a solution on staying dry while you are sailing, or a vacation solution for those sailing trips. If you like great food, you'll get a solution with recipes broken down into a shopping list. This will make the retailer more active and enable the consumer to become more passive, whether the order is given online or in the store.

The exciting part of online advertising and promotion will occur when the Nabisco's of the world put up an Oreo ad on AOL, and that ad leads directly to a Nabisco store powered by NetGrocer or to a brick-and-mortar store that the consumer selects. It will be a Nabisco controlled format with the consumer making the selections as they wish. The advertisement becomes action oriented in a way that the other media channels have never been able to offer. In addition, promotions will be downloaded directly onto the user's computer/or mobile device for future online use or onto the customer's grocery store loyalty card. This card and the value in it will be linked directly into the retailer's point of sales system.

So, what happens to the Krogers and Safeways? Large grocery chains get quite excited about their vegetables, fruits and meats, because that's the fun part of their business. It's where they really deliver value, and it's where they can beat Wal-Mart and the other big box retailers which are their real threat, especially with center of the store non-perishable items. Now, through affiliation with a national e-tailer such as NetGrocer, they have the potential to outsource the center of their store and then focus on what they do best. They should not counter Wal-Mart's Super Centers by building equivalent large boxes with hundreds of thousands of square feet, because then they would be fighting their enemy at their own game. No one can build a box bigger, better, faster and cheaper than Wal-Mart.

The main course of dinner tonight should be the supermarket's business. But what's in my pantry should be the e-retailers business in the form of automated replenishment. Obviously, NetGrocer could become the replenishment and hard-to-find arm of a traditional retailer.

Beyond enabling supermarkets to compete more effectively with the mass merchants and drug chains, the wireless revolution will ensure that access to the e-retailing shopper network will be everywhere. You'll be able to shop and research from anywhere, away from home, on an airplane, wherever it is convenient, and the format will be whatever is easiest for you. And, there will be multiple appliances that will enable you to get into your accounts. Security concerns, as a barrier to shopping, will mostly be solved through biometric identification.

Even when the consumer is in a brick-and-mortar store, wireless devices will allow consumers to be fed targeted promotions based on where they are standing in the store. In addition, the consumer could also source hard-to-find products directly from a kiosk or mobile device while in the store. The irony is that as brick-and-mortar and online retailers merge, most consumers will ignore the concept of traditional versus online sourcing in the same way that they don't care if a traditional store is supplied from a wholesaler or direct from the manufacturer.

One of the implications of wireless is that the consumer is not at home when the purchase is made or to receive delivery. The delivery issue is being addressed by some retailers through the creation of depots or pickup locations, where you can order things online and not have to have them delivered to your office or your home, but have them delivered to a Starbucks or a 7-Eleven, or someone like that. If it's the wrong size, they'll rewrap it, return it, and perhaps charge a small fee. Although it's outside the scope of what many of these locations are used to doing, the issues of storage, pilferage, security, store reformatting, locked rooms, and so on will

be overcome because this is the best way for these retailers to leverage their existing assets with the strengths of the Internet.

As new as the means of e-retailing are, the basic rule of traditional retailing, providing real value to the consumer and to the manufacturer/partner, remains the same. Branding is not a substitute for great merchandising or providing real value to the manufacturers. The exciting question will be which retailers or manufacturers successfully leverage the strengths of this new medium to improve their returns to shareholders. The opportunities are abundant.

hilarybillings

Hilary Billings
Chairman and Chief Marketing Officer

redenvelope

Hilary Billings brings over 14 years of experience in the design and home furnishings industries to her position as Chairman, CMO of RedEnvelope Gifts Online. She joined RedEnvelope after two years as Senior Vice President of Brand Development and Design for Starwood Hotels and Resorts, then the world's largest hotel company. There she initiated a new hotel brand, W Hotels, combining the modern style of a "boutique" hotel with the amenities and services of a business brand. Prior to Starwood, as a Director at Pottery Barn, Billings repositioned the brand by creating an exclusive product line and introducing magazine-style catalog photography. Sales increased to $100 million, making Pottery Barn the most profitable of the Williams-Sonoma Inc. brands. In 1995, Billings became Vice President of Product Design and Development for Pottery Barn Catalog and Retail.

4 web brands

To really understand how and why RedEnvelope got into the e-business and why I am so passionate about our brand, you have to understand where I came from.

Let me take you through the history of what I have done prior to RedEnvelope and how I got here. In the early 1990s, I developed the Pottery Barn brand for Williams-Sonoma. I got there in 1991 and I took over the Pottery Barn business on the catalog side at a time when the Williams-Sonoma group had purchased the Pottery Barn business from the Gap.

In the case of the Pottery Barn in the early 1990s, we saw that there was a home furnishings market that was underserved. If you had disposable income, but didn't want to spend the money on an interior designer in order to have style in your home, there was absolutely nowhere to go. There was a very big market that no retailer was addressing, and yet, there was a significant need among consumers: home furnishing at a good price without having to hire an interior designer.

As director of the catalog for Pottery Barn, I moved the business from tabletop to home furnishings. This was the larger part of the total home business and there was no specialty retailer in that business at that time. The only places to buy home furnishings were large department stores or big furniture stores. If you wanted stylish home furniture, you had to hire an interior decorator because your access to style was only through the trade, and the price points were high. We felt that there was a need for a specialty retail brand focused on style at modest prices. That business grew from $14 million to a $100 million business in the course of four years and became Williams-Sonoma's best margin generating division.

> *"I am a big believer in lifestyle brands, but there are many different kinds of brands. You can only address a certain market by creating a unique product for that market."*

In 1995, I headed up product design development for both the Pottery Barn stores and their catalogs. The combined Pottery Barn business grew to about $500 million in total and became, by far, the leader in specialty home furnishings and the only one for a long time. By now, a few other companies have gotten into this business. Crate & Barrel is more active in home furnishings as well as Restoration Hardware and several others. What was interesting about this experience was not just growing a business, but what the growth of our brand did to change the entire industry.

With the success of Pottery Barn, many of the old-fashioned home furnishing businesses were forced to update. Many of the furniture companies, that were still selling the same style couches, chairs and coffee tables as they had been for years, began to realize that they needed to get on board with a whole new look and feel, because their customers were demanding a lot more fashion from that business. Now, even products like Lazy Boy were concerned about staying current with fashion in their business. So, that was an exciting seven-year period for me.

Then, in 1997, I decided I would like to try to do the same thing again, but in a totally different industry. I went to work for Barry Sternlicht, Chairman of Starwood Hotels and Resorts. Starwood owns Westin and Sheraton and is currently the second largest worldwide hotel company with 650 hotels. Barry Sternlicht was very interested in creating a style brand for the hotel industry, so, together we created W Hotels.

The idea behind W was to address the same void in the hotel business that had existed in the home furnishing business in the early 1990s. The big brand hotels such as Westin and Sheraton were serving the business traveler well from a service perspective, but were way behind from a style perspective. Boutique hotels, such as Ian Schrager Hotels, are addressing the customers' needs from a style and comfort perspective, but, because they are small hotels, they can't really service the business traveler well. In these hotels, you can't get Internet in the rooms and it is hard to get your faxes and your mail on time. And, none of these hotels have any kind of conference facilities for the business traveler.

So, there is a big void to address in the hotel market. W's goal is to bring together a hotel really focused on business needs, but also address this new sophisticated audience of business travelers who are looking for a lot more fashion, style and excitement in their hotel stay.

The name W was born when Starwood had purchased Westin but had not yet purchased Sheraton. W was originally planned to be the fashion sister of the Westin hotels group. Although the name's original tie to Westin was no longer relevant once Starwood bought Sheraton, everyone liked it. So, we kept the name. What was also good about the name was that W allowed us to have a name and a logo all wrapped into one. The idea of just a letter as a name, we thought, was modern and interesting and it worked well.

The hotels had a very active lobby, wonderful down comforters, great showers, big desks and great restaurants. They were fashion focused, but also focused on comfort for the traveler. W was launched with great success. Most of the W hotels run at 95% occupancy which is very high in the hotel business. W is currently the top profit center for the entire Starwood organization.

One of the big challenges in branding is that when a new brand is born – and, in the case of W, it was the first new brand in the hotel industry since the Hyatt was formed 17 years earlier – there is a tremendous amount of focus on it. This creates a real need for educating very large companies about creating something new and taking risks. As W became successful, all the Westin and Sheraton organizations developed a big interest in W, and the focus on innovation slowed down.

When I came to RedEnvelope, I knew I wanted to understand more about how to develop branding inside an e-commerce environment. RedEnvelope is by far the most challenging brand I've ever built. There is *always* a tremendous amount of emotion that's tied to a brand, but getting people to really fall in love with an e-brand requires doing this within an environment of a very small laptop screen. This is a significant challenge.

However, the gift market is a large one and it is underserved. There isn't one upscale, comprehensive gift brand, and so consumers are forced to spend a lot of energy and time in buying a gift. The demographic that we are serving at RedEnvelope, as at W and Pottery Barn, is the young, baby boomer generation between the ages of 30 and 50. These people lead very busy lives. They have a good amount of expendable income and a need for convenience but don't want to trade down in terms of quality and style.

Building the RedEnvelope brand has been an interesting process. We started as 911gifts.com and it was a challenge to convince the founder of the business to change that name. At the time we did this, there was a dot.com belief that you had to say what you did in your name and always had to put dot.com in your name. As a result, you got garden.com, gift.com and book.com and lots more generic dot.com concepts.

We had to convince our company that we ultimately did not want to be just another dot.com business. The Internet was the first place we were going to start – and it would probably be the most important place – but it would have to be a brand that could be extended into any environment important to our customers. We didn't want to have a generic name. We felt that a generic name sold short what our larger vision was for the business. We wanted to build a lifestyle brand with a name that reflected a higher place than just gift.com.

So, we opted for RedEnvelope. Why RedEnvelope? All over Asia, the red envelope signifies a gift. Cash is often put in the envelope or small pieces of jewelry, but what is *in* the envelope is much less important than the fact that when someone hands you a red envelope, it's a gesture of gift giving. That's how we picked the name, RedEnvelope. It signifies that the *gesture* of giving a gift is most important, not just what is inside.

Our customers probably have to buy gifts between 20 and 50 times a year. Everything from a hostess gift to a housewarming gift, to a bereavement gift, and then the traditional Mother's Day and Father's Day holiday gift, and so forth. It is a difficult experience to try and find a gift that's thoughtful, unique, inspiring and interesting, and buy a card and get it wrapped and send it. It is really a cumbersome process.

When we think about the gift business in the US, the interesting thing is that, while in most countries around the world the process of giving and getting a gift is a wonderful, positive experience, many Americans really don't like gift giving. There are many negative associations with giving gifts. People are just overwhelmed by guilt, obligation, and the pressure to impress. Because we are a commercial society, there's a tremendous amount of focus on the *things* we give. This is much more important than the *gesture* of giving and it creates a lot of emotional pressure surrounding gift giving. If we can create the first great gift brand, the higher goal of our business will be to get Americans to learn the benefit of actually enjoying the experience of gift giving, as do many cultures around the world.

While the red envelope is an Asian and not a European tradition, Europeans have that same focus on gift giving as a gesture and a special interaction between two people. We felt that RedEnvelope would be a name that would work well as a global brand, which is what we intend to become.

The color is also a great one with which to build a brand. Red is a color that both men and women like. It is an energetic, passionate color. Nobody in the gift world owns red as a color. In our business, it is the color of Christmas and the color of Valentine's Day. These happen to be two of the biggest gift giving times during the year. Red works very well for us as a color to identify our brand as well as relating to the tradition of the red envelope as a symbol of gift giving.

I also think that our packaging is extremely important. Before the gift is opened, the red wrapping communicates the experience of receiving a gift. How beautifully it is presented is a large part of the total experience. So, our packaging plays a critical role for our business and always will. We have a big photo of our red box right on the home page and this has become an icon for RedEnvelope Gifts Online.

The red envelope concept provides us with a platform on which to build and expand our business. It does not matter what kind of platform your brand is going to use, but there is always a starting point for building a brand. Once you've found that, then it's really a matter of creating an image. RedEnvelope, like Pottery Barn and W, started with identifying an underserved market but then created a lifestyle image around their business.

I believe people need to be excited about the company that they are shopping with. In the hotel industry, people who stay at the W don't even call it a hotel – they just call it the "W". There is an image associated with that and people are excited about this being *their* hotel brand. They don't talk about staying at the Sheraton in quite the same way.

I am a big believer in lifestyle brands, but there are many different kinds of brands. You can only address a certain market by creating a unique product for that market. If you can then layer a real aspiration and lifestyle association with that brand, you really start to see something happening that's special. There are multiple ways of doing that. When you hear someone getting really excited, really proud that the furnishings in their house are from Pottery Barn, or the hotel they are staying at is the W, or the clothes that they wear are from Banana Republic, or any of the other types of lifestyle brands, then you start to create something that is more than just a utility purchasing business.

At RedEnvelope, I believe that to be a great brand we have to be three dimensional to the customer. We are not only an e-brand. We recently launched a catalog and now have a very active catalog business. We are also intending to have stores by next year. The reason that we are doing this is not that we don't think our primary business is always going to be the online environment. But, people tend to shop for gifts at the last minute and they want to shop for them where and when it is convenient to them.

Our feeling is that many times you suddenly realize you need a gift, but you don't want to buy it during lunchtime at the office or in the middle of the night in your pajamas. The online experience is very convenient, but it is hard to create emotional connections solely with a small laptop screen and very small images that still have pretty poor resolution. There are many restrictions to getting people really involved in a brand when your brand is *only* on the Internet.

Many customers today still have to be introduced to the retail brand they love through physical retail, so that they can pick up, touch and smell and be a part of an experience in the store. Their introduction to a brand is thus much more personal and, at this point in time, this is still the best way to get somebody to fall in love with your brand.

We look at the catalog and stores as a strategy to offset our online business. We really look at it as a bridge for the customer today, just to help them fully experience the brand on many levels, while the Internet experience is still at its early stages of development.

But that, I believe, will radically change. I think three years from now, many homes will have a huge screen on their wall that will be fully interactive. This will allow consumers to see a fashion show, point and click and buy that dress right off the fashion show. Consumers will be able to walk virtual aisles in the grocery store. It's going to be an incredible thing. I believe shopping at home, online, will become the most entertaining, interesting avenue to shop and I think it will happen before we know it.

But, in the meantime, we are faced with an environment that is not the easiest in terms of introducing customers to a brand. The Internet is very convenient and I think that there is a great need for this convenience among the customers who are flooding onto it today. Convenience is a huge help to them in their lives and that will be building companies very quickly. What is exciting is that it is moving so fast.

Technology allows the shopping experience to be highly personalized, and to a much greater level than it would be in a store. Soon, I will be able to walk into my favorite online store and the clothes that I would be most interested in because they suit my personality, the kind of clothes I bought before, would be the first things I will see in the store.

Technology has the ability to deliver the kind of personalized experience you couldn't get in a physical environment, or in the mail, and ultimately make it entertaining as well. To really create that same experience that you get in the store, technology will need to create that same environment online. Right now, shopping on the Internet is a very static experience. There's no sound, there's none of the experience you get from all the different sensory levels the way you do in the retail environment. But that will all change.

Most important will be sound and movement. When we will be able to have every product introduction become like a commercial set to wonderful music, we will really start to communicate what that product can do for you in your life. I believe that one of the reasons people feel good in stores is that shopping is really entertaining for people who enjoy shopping. But, you have to go out and do it, and that can be a hassle. If you can have that same kind of entertaining experience at home, it would combine the best of both worlds.

But the number one brand advantage is having your own product that you created. Most manufacturers are very conservative. They are not, for the most part, the ones that are the innovators. The retailers push the manufac- turers to innovate, but they don't do it enough. It is really necessary to take the risk to innovate and create brands that are interesting and more relevant to people. There are people that will argue that. But, I think it's awfully hard, especially through the Internet, to promote a brand that is the same commodity product that everyone else can sell. It's very hard to own your brand and really have a value position that sets you apart from everybody else in a competitive environment, if the product you sell is carried by everybody else. It is critical to have your own branded product line that is better than what is out in the mass market. That, I believe, will continue to be what differentiates great retail brands from each other – online and offline.

There are, of course, retailers, such as Wal-Mart, who market their own brands. But, the problem with these companies is that what they are doing is simply creating versions of the same products that are already in the market. So, whether it's a Wal-Mart's Sam's Choice or Safeway's Safeway Select, it's the same line of products that they have already in their stores, except that they are in their own packaging. They just take their best-selling volume items and put a private brand label on them. Even Neiman Marcus does it. Neiman Marcus will see something selling very well among their high fashion designer brands and they'll create their own version of it.

I don't think that's really serving the customer well. It may be, in the case of Safeway Select, that you can buy Safeway Select Cereal at a better price than Cheerios. There may be an advantage when the store offers products that people really want to buy, but cheaper. What's a lot more interesting to me is to say, "Okay, this is what's available to the consumer in a market, but there is a need for something that no one is providing to them. Let's create a product line that doesn't exist."

In our business category, there are several other gift brands, but their products are not innovative. None, for example, do birthday-specific gifts that are upscale. So, if you want a birthday gift that says "Happy Birthday" on it, your choices are pretty limited. You can buy a bouquet from FTD Flowers or send a big "Happy Birthday" balloon, but it's not that creative, not that interesting and not that upscale. People often have a need to give gifts when someone is very sick or has died. There is no retailer that is focused on really relevant, wonderful, interesting gifts for these very difficult gift purchases.

We are developing gift categories that do not exist in the market anywhere, and, ultimately, we will be giving our customers something that they need, and can't get anywhere else. There are multiple ways to create your own proprietary products. The more interesting way is to create products that do not exist rather than create versions of things that are already out in the market.

I think, for example, that there is a need for a more interesting product line for the corporate gift market. A lot of pens and crystal feature in corporate gift giving because of a lack of innovative products. So, we have an ability to develop this as well, although the consumer brand will always be our primary focus.

We are looking forward to many exciting changes. As technology allows for more creativity, website design will be able to be improved. Right now, we are extremely restricted in the design of our site because of the sheer size of a laptop. But, I think that website design will change greatly in the next few years as this whole medium matures and becomes more sophisticated.

What is most important in e-commerce is that e-businesses make sure that they are focused on an underserved market and that they are addressing the market with something truly, uniquely, their own. If they have that going for them, and they build a good business that is really focused on the needs of their customer, they'll do very well. But many web companies today are not providing a unique web brand for the market. I think that will have to change.

One approach is forming partnerships. Portals, such as AOL or Yahoo!, provide brand distribution. There are still relatively few retail shoppers who are actually shopping online and most of them are coming through a portal. If you are new to the web, you can go to Yahoo! or AOL and they will help to organize the shopping experience for you. Their services have helped many people to find brands for the first time on the web.

Let me comment on one other issue. An article about RedEnvelope in the *New York Times Magazine*, some time ago, was headlined, "The Future is Now or Never." I think that the journalist played into the fashion of the Internet at that time when companies were rushing into the Internet because they believed that it is now or never.

But that is not a good e-branding philosophy. Web brands must be very concerned with long range loyalties and must focus on the long-term vision for their brand. They must be aware how important it is to have a long-term mission, building the right foundation for their business and communicating with their customers.

There are many ways of doing this. Most importantly, we are making sure that our customers can communicate with us any way they want. We have an 800 number available 24 hours a day; we have live chat, right on the system; we have email available to make sure that we can connect with a customer at any time, anywhere. We have an organization that makes sure that operationally we can say to a customer that we're going to be able to ship a gift overnight and that we will get it there on time. All these different parts of creating an e-business are crucial to building the foundation the first time we start doing business with a customer. As the brand grows, we must be prepared to really deliver the promise, because ultimately a brand is a promise that you make to the customer. The responsibility of a company to their customers is to always deliver on their promise to them.

It is surprising how similar this is to the other businesses in which I have been involved. Almost everything is the same. The main difference has been that RedEnvelope's primary platform is the Internet. But, while the Internet is still at an early stage of development today, it is necessary to extend ourselves in many different ways to connect with the customer.

Most people are working hard and are trying to spend more time at home. If they can do more of their shopping at home in a way that is exciting and gives them better information about the services, I believe this will become the primary way they will shop. I do not think physical retail will go away and I don't think that direct mail will go away. But, the growth of online shopping keeps breaking records, and I believe it will continue to grow at a tremendous rate. I am convinced that e-commerce will be the most important shopping channel in the next five years and that e-brands such as RedEnvelope will take center stage in that environment.

deborahchae andybateman

Deborah Chae
President
Andy Bateman
Managing Director

interbrandinteractive

Deborah Chae is the President and Global Managing Director of Interbrand Interactive, and has 15 years of experience and leadership in online and offline branding. Her early career included experience with brand consulting firms SBG Partners and Landor Associates as a senior account director working with corporate clients in the US and the Asia-Pacific. Prior to joining Interbrand, Chae helped found Novo Interactive, one of the first strategic online consultancies in the US. As a co-founder, she helped grow the business from its inception to a staff of over 300 people in its San Francisco office. Novo consistently has earned "Top Interactive Agency" honors from *Adweek* and *Advertising Age*.

Andy Bateman is Managing Director of Interbrand Interactive and has spent the past 12 years understanding, building and rebuilding brands to face and build relationships with ever-changing customers and environments. He was classically trained in advertising with WCRS in London, managing brands which included Forte Hotel Group, Grand Metropolitan, Carling Beers, NEC Corporation, Lotus and Dell Computers. Bateman created the first strategic planning group for DDB Rapp Collins in Sydney, Australia and later for WPP group's creative boutique, Batey Kazoo. Prior to joining Interbrand Interactive, he moved to the US as part of the team charged with the transformation and repositioning of J Walter Thompson New York.

5 the strategic role of e-branding

Thanks also to Diane Hong, Jez Frampton and Mina Park for their help with this chapter.

The Internet dichotomy

It has been a fascinating time to be in business. This period has been called everything from the modern-day gold rush to the new economy to the information revolution. We have seen the rise of the knowledge worker and the demise of many Internet start-ups. The streets of Silicon Valley are littered with pink slips and tattered business plans, but those same streets are filled with numerous Internet millionaires walking to their empires.

It has also been a fascinating time to be alive. The Internet has made true its promise to permeate and change our lives. Are we more connected or more isolated? From the early days of The Well, the Internet has made possible connections and interconnections that grow into a wonderful web community. It has facilitated online support groups for those who previously had no access. It has brought the world closer to us, yet we sit at our computers removed from this world. We do our banking online. We have our groceries and videos delivered to our door in an hour. We find ourselves interacting with people less and less. We are so tied to our cell phones, beepers and talking appliances that it is difficult to have a quiet moment with oneself.

> *"Brands are actually asking, 'What is it that you need? I'll go and get it for you.'"*

And how does all of this affect brands? Are brands more important or less important in e-space? In a world where bargain hunters seek out the cheapest product, and comparison sites can lead you through decision making, consumers may not seem as loyal to product or retailer. However, while in our perpetual information overload, brands can serve as the lighthouse, shining bright in the sea of clutter. How to navigate branding in this new world is one of the most important issues facing our clients today.

Definition of terms

E-branding has taken on a couple of popular usages. The first is to represent the marketing efforts of pure play Internet brands. When writing the words "pure play," we realize that the term has already started losing meaning. These brands that originated on the Internet are not just contained within the Internet. They are merging with traditional companies, morphing into different forms for different gadgets, and, as with so many aspects of life, they cannot remain "pure" for very long.

The other common usage of e-branding really refers to e-marketing. When Hot Wired created the first banner ad in 1994, marketers started to realize that they had a whole new medium to consider, one that required new kinds of creativity, that sought to interact with consumers, one that needed a new term altogether.

E-marketing brought to the forefront a key issue for all brands – the relationship with the customer. After years of running television spots for the masses, marketers were able to target specific ads to specific customers and even send personalized email. After sending out volumes of direct mail with 1% response rates, marketers were finding that interested customers wanted to interact with their websites page after hyper-linked page. Suddenly, consumers were able to find all sorts of information, sometimes more information than companies felt comfortable sharing themselves. Car buyers were empowered with knowing the Blue Book value of cars prior to negotiation. Consumers were swapping stories about their experiences. Many debates ensued about one-on-one marketing and privacy, but the exciting news was that the customer was simply a click away.

Branding, in its "purest" sense, incorporates aspects of both popular usages, but encompasses much more. Yes, the Internet, as part of the marketing mix, is an important component of branding – but it is one component. Yes, Internet brands have certain considerations particular to them, but all companies must ask themselves what strategic role their brand must play in their respective businesses. In the early days of e-commerce, Internet brands witnessed that some important roles brands must fulfill online were to provide familiarity and trust, so that consumers would feel safe shopping online. First, we will examine the list of questions any organization should ask itself to determine the role of brand. Only when it has determined *what* should be accomplished can the organization decide *how* to accomplish it.

The strategic role of a brand

All companies should ask themselves a series of questions to discern the role their brand will play. As a business asset, brands should fulfill business goals and be measured, in part, based on those goals. The following questions are a starting point to arrive at the ultimate answer. These types of question simply help to facilitate the discussions that should happen at management level about the brand.

- *What business are you in?*
  What business will you be in five years from now?
  This may be a seemingly straightforward question, but you would be surprised at the varying answers you receive from different people within your organization. If you are a research company, some internal constituents may think you are in the information business, others may think you are in technology, still others may think you are a knowledge service business.

  Agreement is necessary in order to answer the next question and define the competition and your place among the competition.

- *What are the drivers of your business – will those drivers change?*
  What drives purchase and loyalty in your business? Perhaps what used to drive the business is changing and is now just a cost of entry.

How do you see these drivers changing and how are you positioned to deliver these drivers?

Is there an opportunity to create a new driver that you can own?

How well do competitors fulfill those drivers?
Evaluate your competition and what it is they offer. To build on the above example of the research company, perhaps your primary competitor delivers on speed. How important is speed to *your* customer base? How do you deliver on speed versus your competition? Do you want to compete on this driver or try to own quality instead? Is speed a sustainable proposition, given the online competitors?

What about emerging competitors? How might they surprise you?

What does your brand currently represent to customers?
Perhaps your brand doesn't represent anything to your customers and it is the individual sales representatives that have drawn in the customer base. Look at your customer research. Talk to different customers and potential customers. If the brand equals nothing or even has some negative baggage, there is much work to do.

Perhaps what you represent are no longer important drivers in the industry. If you are lucky enough to represent relevant drivers, how can you keep your message fresh and meaningful?

What do you want your brand to represent to customers?
Think not only of the drivers of the business but of your company as a whole. What do you want them to think of your products and services? Is there a gap between current perceptions and where you would like to be?

How do you want them to view you as a company? How do you want them to describe your relationship with them? Strong brands have distinct personalities and also inspire loyalty.

■ *How many brands are there in your brand portfolio?*
How are they organized?
Assess your marketing budgets and think about how expensive it is to
maintain a brand. How many brandable products/services do you
really have? Does your customer understand how your brands are
organized?

Your brands should be organized to relay the depth of your offering
and to relay the interrelationship between offerings, but they often just
mimic organizational structures.

■ *Where does the primary brand equity lie (for example, corporate level,*
product level)?
Is it where you want the value to be?
Where does the customer hold the most value in your company? Is it
with a certain product when you ultimately want it to be at the
corporate level? If so, how can you start moving the equity up to build
the corporate brand? This may call for some new brand architecture
and nomenclature.

■ *Where are the growth opportunities for your business?*
What are the possible new revenue streams? Where is the industry
moving? How can you lead the change versus simply follow it?

■ *Where does the brand have to stretch for future growth?*
Your brand planning should take into consideration growth opportunities and any upcoming merger and acquisition activity. The brand
positioning needs to be elastic enough to allow for your future growth.

A company's brand should be based on a thorough assessment of its
business and given certain ambitions to fulfill. The brand strategy can then
be used proactively against competitors and ensure future success.

"True understanding comes from practice itself" – Zen teaching

After assessing the strategic role of brand, the challenge is then to make the seemingly complex simple. Every good brand starts with a big idea: a core idea that differentiates it from the competition, that is based on its strengths, that is meaningful to its customers, and is elastic enough to allow for future growth. It is on this core idea that the company's foundation is based. The corporate mission and values should support the brand promise. Each department and every employee within each department should know the role they play in the success of the brand.

The brand should have a road map to route the ways in which it will accomplish all that it strategically needs to accomplish. It should have a plan outlined on how to build the best relationship possible with its customers. It should have a process in place so that the brand resonates clearly and consistently internally, externally and in every environment, including the Internet.

Brands and the Internet environment

The irony of the Internet is that as it makes us all more connected, it is at the same time less personal, using GUIs (graphic user interfaces), and not people, to represent customer interactions before, during and after sales. This makes Internet interactions mission-critical, and brands exponentially more important in delivering a unique and engaging customer experience. So, as the market for Internet development shifts from construction to content, from systems integration to engineering applications, from low bandwidth HTML to bandwidth-intensive rich media sites, and from PC converged to diverged wireless platforms, there is a clear opportunity for a new type of brand and a new type of branding practice.

When we talk about e-brands, we think that the "e" prefix pertains more to a changed environment for brands rather than merely an electronic version. Brands are still brands, but the new environment – let's call it the Internet – is currently the most pervasive manifestation for a cyberworld in which we're all connected across a wide variety of appliances. It is so profoundly different from the physical world as to warrant a new role for brands, new ways to brand, and therefore a piece of code to represent the new era for brands – e-branding.

Let me offer an analogy to illustrate how profoundly different we think the Internet environment is for brands. Let's imagine that you're a large US or Europe-based business and you want to expand your business globally, since you've grown all that you can grow domestically. If global trading was representative of the Internet, then we think that it would be as profoundly different an environment as if the only other language and culture outside your country was Chinese. Clearly, to succeed globally, you'd have to learn a new language, a new set of social customs, and perhaps even be subject to market conditions that require a rethink of your business model. You might even need to teach your staff the Chinese way. You would be missing an opportunity if you didn't try to accommodate these new global customers' needs. When you put it like this, it's surprising that so many companies who have tried to extend their business and their brands onto the Internet have neglected to learn the new language and appear to simply force fit their brands into new environments. Evidence is mounting that this simply doesn't work.

The control that customers have today is also forcing brands to be honest, because you're collapsing the whole process of purchase. You can go from awareness right through to purchase and also repurchase in the one environment, the one space. So as a consumer, I may know how much the seller paid for that part and how much profit they are going to make on it. There are enough sources of information, all in one place, for me to know a lot about the brand.

We can identify seven best practices for e-brands, or e-branding.

Ceding control

First, ceding control is perhaps the most contentious. Internet and Internet technologies have allowed organizations to offer up some control on behalf of the user to product, price, place and promotion. For example, Dell decided that they can actually give up the configuration of their products and give that to consumers so that you can configure your Dell computer exactly the way you want to configure it. In a very real sense, Dell has ceded control to customers over product. The result is currently $45 million a day in sales, plus a reduced inventory holding – everybody wins!

Seeing that success as a brand online is borne of the fact that rather than subscribe, or ask consumers to subscribe, to advertising messages to make their purchase decisions, companies have actually allowed other users to comment on the product's capabilities as a key form of promotion. So that in fact they've given away promotion. Brands that are featured on CNet actually pay to be featured and written about by consumers – good or bad. Quite a turnaround from the push-based communications industry. Similarly too, Mercata has decided that on a grand scale, if they club together lots of buyers, they might be able to drive prices down. Priceline has been an early player in this market, but the likes of eBay and Mercata might be the ones that survive in the long term, since they have really ceded control of price to users. So ceding control is an enormously powerful new lever for branding in the new economy.

Community participation

Another powerful new lever for branding is community participation. If you read through the pages of the introduction to Cisco's Annual Report, you'll see that Cisco, rather than a collection of companies, considers itself an ecosystem where each company feeds off another, where customers, in fact, feed off Cisco and Cisco feeds off customers. The notion that you can create and participate in communities is unique to the Internet. And, it is a unique lever for brands in terms of generating credibility and relevance and even differentiation. It's incumbent on e-brands to both participate in other communities and to create communities for themselves, thereby extending the footprint of the brand.

Even commodity brands will have to rethink their role and rethink the business they are in. Kimberly-Clark makes tissues, toilet paper, sanitary napkins and babies' diapers. Where is the opportunity? In the diaper business, the opportunity is in how to toilet train, and this is a way to develop a relationship with consumers. There are a number of solutions to the problems of growing up, and by stepping back to see how they could be more helpful, not just through their product line, but by becoming more information oriented, Kimberly-Clark offers more solutions to more people.

Fostering dialogue with users

The third principle, or rule of engagement, seems to be about fostering real dialogue with users, customers and suppliers, rather than "shiny marketing-speak." It is clear that the Internet offers an opportunity for users to participate directly in a company's actions. There are as many sites dedicated to discrediting IBM as there are sites created by IBM. So it's clear that customers have a voice, and they will act as activists if they're not given that voice. You really need to foster true dialogue, not marketing dialogue, with customers and users. And with those brands that do seem to be more successful. They ask for input, listen to their customers and act on their customers' advice. Look at MTV – a brand that has built incredible value over a short time by understanding and giving a voice to a generation of young people.

Focus on the core competency

The fourth area is focus. Clearly, a lot of the brands that have been more successful have "stuck to their knitting." They have decided that their core competency is what they will focus on in their Internet offering, but they will cooperate and collaborate with other partners to round out that offering and turn products into services. Yahoo! is a good example. They don't claim to be in finance, or in messaging, news or shopping, but they have partnered with other experts so that they can focus on their core discipline of connecting people to the Internet while allowing others on their site to participate and create a better branded offering for Yahoo!

Deliver good ideas

The fifth principle is probably the simplest, but also the most difficult to deliver. And that's about having good ideas. If we're going to encourage people to change their behavior, to shop online, transact online and meet online, then they have to be given a good reason to do so. Your brand, in fact, has to have a good idea behind it, because frankly, dealing with the offline world isn't much of a problem for most people. They've learned to do it generation through generation. Having a good idea for your brand is going to be important. AOL has a good idea. They connect you very, very simply to the Internet. As an appliance, it's very easy to use. eBay has a good idea. It's a very good idea. But of course, no good idea is a good idea for long, unless it remains current and relevant.

Keep your content current

Having timely and relevant content is the sixth principle, or rule of engagement, for branding in this economy. It's not enough anymore to provide news. That news has to be served up fast and has to be deeply insightful. It's not enough to provide a basic service. You must consistently add to that service and make your content current. As the Internet moves into a phase of differentiating not by basic functionality, it moves into more of a content-based role. We're already starting to see the grains of that, where brands are competing, not based on what they do, but rather on the content of what they do. So currency of that content is critical. The online trading marketplace is no longer about real-time online transactions; it's about advice and guidance, analysis and insight.

The experience must be engaging

The final rule of engagement is simply this – engagement. Right now, the Internet is one of the most difficult to navigate and dull experiences that you can probably have with a computer. Strangely enough, most websites look like reinterpreted Microsoft Windows applications. Not surprisingly, because most of the programmers who created those sites were, in fact, programmers for software just like Microsoft Windows. But that's not enough for increasingly demanding users and customers. The digital environment is one of the most sensuous environments on earth. We can have touch, we can have voice, video, graphics and text all merged and converged in one environment. In some cases now, we can also have smell on the Internet through smart applications that you can add to your PC. So it's critical that if this medium, this environment, is going to compete with other multimedia environments like video games, like television and like the real world, then the experience must be very, very engaging. It must be sticky. So brands that are going to be successful are those that are going to have engaging, rich, interesting things to say.

Those seven rules again: ceding control, community participation, fostering real dialogue, focusing on core competencies, having good ideas and having and maintaining current and engaging content. These are the equity levers that are newly available to brands that leverage technology.

The Internet is a perfect environment in which to leverage this new role. The role is what we'll call the Genie. Where the Genie grants you at least three wishes and probably many more and where brands are actually asking, "What is it that you need? I'll go and get it for you." Some good examples here are Yahoo!, AOL, Virgin, and in some ways, even MTV. It's not about Internet brands necessarily, but it is about brands in the new economy, acting as guides for customers.

We are finding that, just as in the old economy, brands are the source of sustainable, competitive advantage in the new economy. Real value is only derived through whole user experiences with products, price, place, people and promotion. Some of these experiences represent real value and provide for differentiation between competitors.

The future looks bright for brands; a new economy has created a new set of equity levers to pull, a new relationship, an increasingly critical role as the only point of contact.

Through all this, a strong brand begins with a strong center and emanates from that core. Brand stewards know that branding takes vigilance and consistency. Branding is an active discipline that requires work and a common understanding shared by all parts of the corporation regarding their greater whole, their brand. Regardless of the environment, it could be the Internet Age today and an entirely different one tomorrow, these core principles remain the same.

So is the brand more or less important in the Internet space? It is for you to answer, as your actions will make it a self-fulfilling prophecy.

viviennebechtold

Vivienne Lee Bechtold
Director of I-Knowledge

procter&gamble

Vivienne Lee Bechtold is Director of I-Knowledge for Procter & Gamble. In 1999, Bechtold was recognized by industry publication *Advertising Age* as "Interactive Marketer of the Year." Bechtold has had previous experience within the P&G marketing department working in the Beauty Care Sector and as a Brand Manager in P&G's Haircare Worldwide Strategic Planning organization. In 1997, she co-founded the P&G interactive team to leverage the Internet and other new media to build P&G's businesses. In 1998, under her leadership, P&G hosted the FAST Summit, the industry-wide conference that tackled the tough Internet issues facing big advertisers. She now has responsibility for leading P&G's overall Internet strategy.

6 the dynamics for package goods on the internet

With the mainstream growth of the Internet and electronic media over the past few years, new "i" and "e" words are being coined all the time, but different people may have slightly different interpretations of the same words. So for clarity, the definition of "e-branding" used in this chapter is when a brand's identity and equity is extended onto the Internet, or through electronic media. This involves synergizing both physical and digital assets in such a way that the brand is consistent online and offline, and consumers are not confused but see the brand as one holistic brand.

This chapter focuses on the impact of the Internet and e-branding on consumer package goods. That said, some of the business dynamics and opportunities may be reapplicable to other businesses and some will be unique to package goods. First, we'll touch on the role of brands and the Internet; second, we'll share some initial learning and educated assertions about web shopping for consumer package goods, and third, we'll cover key areas of impact.

Brands play an important role on the Internet since they are a key source of trust and confidence for consumers. Many believed that the Internet opened up the opportunity for every "mom and pop" business to sell their products online, and we do see some of that. But, since people cannot see, touch or feel the actual product online, having a strong brand and strong equity along with high awareness becomes a key factor to Internet success.

For example, in the online grocery shopping experience, people generally do not buy private labels, because they simply don't have the trust and confidence that they have with familiar branded products. Because of this overall brand awareness, the number one and number two brands in any given product category will have a disproportionate advantage on the Internet, especially if they give support to the trust and confidence of the consumer.

> *"Since people cannot see, touch or feel the actual product online, having a strong brand and strong equity, along with high awareness, becomes a key factor to Internet success."*

For that reason, the e-branding opportunity is generally best served when both online and offline assets are involved. The two parts work together to reinforce the best each has to offer. Although there are exclusively online businesses such as the Amazons of the world, they will be more the exception than the rule. In most business categories, the Barnes & Noble bookstore model, where the brand has both an online presence and reputable brick-and-mortar stores, will be the stronger model.

However, the Internet offers new ways for new brands to be introduced by leveraging the Internet. This will be especially true with package goods. Think about the dynamics when a brand is trying to plan a national or international rollout and trying to achieve the right timing of when to turn on the marketing support to match the distribution rollout. Traditionally, if the marketing support is too late, retailers have products sitting on their shelves and not moving, because people don't know about the brand yet. And if the marketing effort is turned on too early, consumers are disappointed when they hear about the brand, go to the store to buy it, and find the brand is not available yet.

By introducing new brands on the Internet, companies can take advantage of seeding, or building early awareness and trial for a new brand by selling it online before it is available for purchase more broadly. This develops a grass-roots user base prior to getting broad scale national distribution in the stores. Brands can develop and keep people's interest early on and then use it as part of the test market process to test the effectiveness of different components of the marketing plan. In fact, test markets themselves are changing quite dramatically. A softer, fuzzier launch process becomes more the norm. Products will go from seeding, then some iteration of seeding and testing, right into a broad scale launch because of the Internet.

Seeding of new brands and identifying people who are interested in the brand's proposition fits well with the Internet. And, in many cases, early adopters of new brands are people who find the brand or category particularly meaningful. Once they use the product, they become supporters for the brand in terms of passing along the information and endorsement to their friends and getting the word out virally. This effect can be positive or negative, depending on their opinion of the brand. But seeding enables the brand to get the awareness up among people who have a predisposition for using the brand.

Lest anyone be confused that I am advocating that brands should be marketing solely through the Internet, I am not. Online marketing cannot do it alone. Even dot.coms have learned this lesson, as evidenced by the amount of TV, outdoor, print and radio ads that support dot.com brands. For example, if the brand wants to get broad reach, or establish visual or emotional equity, it's much easier and more effective to use some offline medium options, such as TV or print, to reach the target audiences. At this point, it's very difficult to replicate online what TV can do in terms of creating an emotional connection with consumers. But, if the objective is to provide cost-effective customer care or target different consumers with different messages or propositions, nothing beats the Internet. In today's environment, it really requires a good mix of TV, radio, print, Internet, in-store, and so on to achieve all of a brand's marketing objectives.

Effective new brand introductions can take advantage of very complementary uses of online and offline, such as Procter & Gamble experienced with the Physique launch. Physique was a new hair care brand that Procter & Gamble launched in 2000. The brand created and ran 15-second teaser ads that built awareness about Physique coming prior to its launch and directing people to its website www.physique.com. The TV spots were focused on building a visual and emotional equity for Physique, and the website was used to give more info about the line-up of products. When consumers went to the website, they could find out more about the products that were going to be available and could opt in and receive samples. Not only could consumers receive samples, but also they could "refer a friend" to receive samples or sign up to become part of "Club Physique" and receive regular news and tips via email from the Physique brand. This is a good example of how TV and the Internet complemented each other. Synergizing offline and online gives the brand the opportunity for the marketing to become stronger.

The global influence of the Internet will also affect package goods brands marketing strategy. E-branding immediately requires a brand to act like a global brand, even if it's not in distribution in all parts of the world today, because consumers all over the world will have access to it. It may start with the website, but there are also implications such as global packaging, a global look, and a global brand character since people will see the brand in this global environment. Before its extension onto the Internet, the brand and the visual identity via packaging may have stood for one thing in one country, and another thing in another country and this may not have been a big deal. But because of the Internet, brands that will succeed must reconcile the differences and put more emphasis on establishing a common identity, equity, and character that consumers can recognize and relate to all over the world.

Manufacturers will have to think more about global launches, or quick global rollouts, because through word of mouth and consumer interest, demand for the brand may exceed availability. For example, when Procter & Gamble launched Crest White Strips, a product for whitening teeth, on the Internet, the product was available initially only in the US. But, through word of mouth, people from other countries began contacting the brand to ask when it was going to be available outside the US.

Let's move onto the topic of web shopping for package goods products and review some initial learning. There are three things that will make online shopping different among the different package goods categories such as food, beauty care, health, laundry and so forth. First, there is a greater degree of customization that people would like in certain categories and the Internet provides the opportunity. For example, if I'm crazy about red M&Ms, M&M/Mars can provide me with the opportunity to purchase packages of just red M&Ms ... or green M&Ms ... or M&M packages that don't contain any brown ... or whatever was meaningful for consumers. For laundry detergents, the need for customization may not be as obvious, but think about water hardness, fragrance preferences, level of fragrance preference, and types of cleaning needs which might encourage people to want a higher degree of customization if they could get it. However, with a category such as toilet paper, I'm not sure how customized people really want to get!

Second, online shopping will be different depending on the degree of consumer comfort with the product category. Research has shown that the closer the product is to impacting a person physically, the more cautious people are about buying it online. For example, if a consumer is going to eat or ingest something, which would be very close and personal, it would probably be a harder sell to get people to buy that kind of product online than it would be in a brick-and-mortar environment. Whereas if that same consumer was buying laundry detergent where the laundry detergent only affects her clothes – it touches her outer skin only – she might have a greater degree of comfort. Therefore, the online experience will be different, depending on the consumer comfort with the product category.

The third variable is the degree of variability among the purchased products. There is a greater degree of variability in clothing than in a CD or book. Not all white cotton sweaters are made the same – not only the feel of the fabric, but also the size and the detailing. The greater the degree of variance in the product, the more difficult the online shopping experience, versus a product that has less variable such as Cheerios. Here's a box of Cheerios and it's always the same product, so consumers are more likely to be comfortable ordering it online. Package goods that have a greater degree of variability are probably harder to sell initially, but once people get over that hurdle, they may be comfortable having others pick out things for them. So package goods online will have different shopper attitudes based on the degree of customization, consumer comfort, and the variance in the product itself.

There are a number of considerations that could greatly enhance the web shopping experience and here are just a few thought starters:

1   Let's consider whether consumers' packaging needs and expectations of an e-retailer are different from that of a grocery store for consumer package goods. For example, it seems logical that the needs and expectations of consumers should be different, just as there are

different sizes and selections featured at a grocery store versus a drug store versus a mass merchandiser. In the club store business, consumers want club packs of larger sizes, or bundled packs that gave people more bulk and better value. Club store shoppers' habits and practices indicated that people shopped less frequently but bought larger sizes or bigger quantities so club packs were created to conform with the way people shop and stock up.

In the e-retailing environment, there will be some sort of similar dynamics and similar expectations based on consumers' habits and practices. With e-grocers, particularly for package goods, buying is probably done more on a weekly basis since there is a need for fresh products that cannot be stocked up. The value need is probably not based on larger sizes, but at the same time, the e-shopper is looking for value. So packaging might not be a new physical package, but it might be a type of orderable package. For example, consumers could order a 10-pack of Pampers diapers, which is much larger than the normal individual packs that someone would buy. But consumers would not order them to be delivered at the same time. They could have them delivered two at a time, or one per week for the next ten weeks (whatever fits their habits and practices), but pay for them all at a time in order to get the bulk rate. Manufacturers will probably be willing to take a smaller margin per individual package, in order to get consumers to lock into a higher overall purchase upfront and take those consumers out of the market for the next four weeks.

Another approach would be to "buy a certain number of packages, get one free." Since it's relatively easy to keep track of purchases online, consumers could buy Pampers this week, then next week, and so forth, once they hit the fifth time they could get a free pack of Pampers. It's a way of getting people to lock in upfront, commit to buying the product, getting it delivered over a five-week period, and either getting the sixth one free in that context, or getting a lower overall rate on the five that they bought. Therefore, package size needs can and will change for e-retailing versus conventional retailing.

2   Beyond package size, another consideration is how brands will provide consumers with more information about the products that they receive. The Internet provides the opportunity to convey this information and many consumers will want it, especially with new brands. E-retailers are challenged to develop a shopping environment or experience environment where consumers can easily find the package goods products they are looking for. Packaging on the Internet can become an important contributor to brand recognition. In the e-retail environment, the package is often the first visual encounter you have with the product and it becomes the "face" of the brand and its link to product information. The package has the potential to become a recognizable icon that brings the brand to life, emphasizing the important attributes of the product such as appetite appeal and product usage. E-retailers need to find a way of showing the products and communicating the key elements and information from the packaging in a way that effectively uses the medium, so it doesn't overwhelm the consumer with unnecessary information. This includes specific versions, specific flavors, specific sizes and even ingredient statements when they don't have a physical product in hand. They need to make it an easy visual experience and ensure that the written translation of the package is easy for the consumer to interface with.

As an industry, progress is being made towards the development of some information standards resulting in a global equity database. The concept involves manufacturers supplying visuals of their packages and specific product information, enabling retailers to have a common database of information to draw from. For example, e-retailers globally could pull out the standard information for a 13 oz. bottle of Pantene normal version shampoo. And this would include the SKU code, visuals of the product, ingredient statement for that package, and any other back panel information that might be of use to the consumer or retailer. There is still a lot of experimenting to see how e-retailers will choose to show that information within their interface, but it provides a common source of information.

3   A third consideration for package goods and web shopping is optimizing how package goods can take advantage of the Internet through bundling or logical cross-selling. If consumers' habits and practices indicate that they tend to purchase certain kinds of products together, those items could be more effectively bundled or located together. For example, baby wipes could be placed on a "virtual shelf" that also contains paper towels and other kinds of paper clean-up products. Or they could also be placed with other baby products. Or why not both! In a physical grocery store, they would be found in one or maybe two places since stores don't want to have the same product in multiple aisles for efficiency of stocking. But in a virtual store environment, the same product could actually be placed in multiple places, wherever it might make sense to the consumer. The challenge then becomes one of understanding the consumer's shopping preferences to determine how different categories of products ought to be organized within the shopping environment.

4   Package goods selection could be further customized without over-whelming consumers. Today, a physical store may be limited to four versions of a particular hair conditioner for space/cost efficiency. At the same time, product testing might indicate that selecting from six versions (covering a broader range of needs) could actually signifi-cantly increase consumer satisfaction for people that are on the high and low ends of conditioning needs. In an e-retailing environment where shelf space is less of an issue, a retailer could offer all six versions, or better yet, a consumer would have the option of indicating that they only want to see the versions of each brand designed for color treated hair. Taking this one step further, consumers should be able to see only the categories that are of interest to them. People

who do not own pets do not need to see pet products during most visits because it is simply not relevant to them. This will improve the consumer shopping experience by not overwhelming consumers with information overload and having more choices. It could actually reduce the complexity of their selection process and increase consumer satisfaction with the products they eventually purchase.

5   The shopping experience for package goods could be enhanced on the Internet by creating utilities that make the decision-making process easier. For example, take a look at the feminine care category. When people get to the feminine care aisles and are faced with choices of different protection levels of pads, tampons and whatever, it's difficult to shop. They often don't know what they need and often walk away with a package that is not really the best product to meet their specific needs. By building online utilities at the point of decision making, it would aid consumers in helping to pick particular products that meet their particular needs.

6   New-to-the-world products are often introduced in the physical store by placing the packages in floor stands or displays in prominent store locations with high traffic, such as at the end of an aisle or where shoppers first enter the store. Since these brands, and sometimes these product categories, often have never existed before, no one is actually looking for them. The idea is to get shoppers to stop and look at the new products, interrupting their shopping experience. In an e-retailing environment, new approaches can be developed to introduce new brands or products. For example, e-retailers can group all the new products in a special new products area so that when people begin their online shopping experience, or when they are finished with their regular shopping, they are guided through the new brands selection to view new brands and products which they may not be familiar with or which only recently came into distribution.

7   Impulse buying could be different online. We know that certain package goods categories, such as sodas and salted snacks, are driven by impulse purchases. Once again, e-retailers could replicate this type of impulse buying through bundling on the virtual store shelves, where the snacks might be near other products that would trigger a similar impulse.

8   A final thought for package goods shopping on the web is the whole idea of a shopping list for replenishment. There are some package goods products that consumers know they buy week in and week out. Wouldn't it be great to walk into a physical store and have a shopping basket waiting there, already containing those items? Then all consumers would have to do is shop for the smaller list of special things. Well, consumers can do just that online today.

The list of web shopping implications could go on, but let's stop here and move on to some broader implications of e-branding for consumer package goods.

First, it will be important for package goods companies to gain marketing spending efficiencies by the Internet. One important method will be by focusing on the high potential consumers, those with high category consumption and high loyalty. Without the Internet, many advertisers have broadcasted their messages in a way that assumes everyone should be treated about the same. This occurs with TV advertising, coupons, and many other offline marketing efforts. But, with the advent of the Internet, advertisers are starting to ask, "Who are my best customers (or consumers), what would add the most value for them, and how can we service them in a way that rewards their loyalties differently from someone who is not brand loyal or who is a switcher for other reasons?"

Another efficiency would be to focus on brand retention and increasing and extending usage across the line of products. This goes back to knowing who the best customers are, and getting them to buy the brand one more time instead of buying a competitive brand, so they can buy the brand ten out of twelve times instead of only eight out of twelve times. Or they buy other products within the same brand to meet a spectrum of needs. This can often equate to a very significant business opportunity. For example, through retention, someone who uses Vidal Sassoon conditioner is probably a great target to try Vidal Sassoon styling products.

We know that consumer research on the Internet can be huge. Package goods brands spend a lot of money on consumer research, and it can often be done faster, better and cheaper through the Internet. By leveraging web-based research package goods manufacturers can get their products into the market faster, hopefully meet consumer needs better, and provide more real-time responsiveness.

In certain categories, the value proposition for consumers is such that they are willing to pay for products that are customized for them, and that is the concept behind Reflect.com, which offers a personalized beauty experience. Does that mean that Reflect.com will put Cover Girl and Max Factor and other cosmetics brands out of business? Not likely. Not everyone will find the customization opportunity a high enough value to pay for the higher prices required. But a segment of consumers will find customization important enough to pay willingly for it, and it can become a new revenue stream and opportunity for new business models.

We are also starting to see package goods companies extending their brands and their offerings into the service area, so that they're not just selling physical goods, but they're actually providing or selling complimentary services to go with them.

Package goods companies and brands are just beginning to understand how new digital devices can offer new, more engaging e-branding opportunities. On the marketing front, consumers can experience greater engagement with brands in interactive environments than from sitting on the couch and passively watching a 30-second commercial roll by. Early learning from experiments with in-store kiosks and ads on interactive TV suggests there is a huge opportunity and interest in this area.

On the wireless front, package goods manufacturers have been experimenting with a wide variety of e-devices. Most folks have heard about Coke's experience using the cell phone to pay for vending machine purchases. That can affect the entire soft drink category, enabling the category to be in more places and eliminating the consumer need for cash to make a purchase. And, wouldn't it be great if the laundry brand package that consumers buy from the store could actually talk to their washing machine and the clothes they've thrown into the machine, link to a stain detector utility from the Internet, and enable the washing machine to set itself to provide the best wash for each load of laundry? Or, what if the refrigerator could have the scanning capability to know which products/ brands it contains? It could then access the Internet to suggest recipes that could be made with the available products. These are only a few ideas for wireless devices in the future and they are not so far off.

Even very stable, traditional product categories, such as package goods, are significantly impacted by what information technology and the Internet can offer. People should not think that technology only makes a difference in dot.com companies and technology-based companies, since package goods servicing is a big opportunity and, undoubtedly, huge change will continue to unfold before us. Undoubtedly, package goods companies should keep experimenting with new ideas for e-branding. Mark Twain once said, "Continuous improvement is better than delayed perfection." Consumer package goods companies have to be willing to test, measure results, and then keep advancing their learning. Through experimentation and fast cycle learning, e-branding will continue to evolve and become an even more powerful part of the marketing mix.

charlesbrymer

Charles E. Brymer
Group Chief Executive

interbrandgroup

Charles E. (Chuck) Brymer is Group Chief Executive of the Interbrand Group. He is responsible for managing Interbrand's global interests and enhancing the company's offerings to clients. Chuck began his career at BBDO, then joined Interbrand in 1985 as the President of its US operations and became Group Chief Executive of the Interbrand Group in 1993. He has been instrumental in the strategic development of the company's business, and has personally supervised branding and identity programs for MCI, Compaq, Samsung, Discover, Procter & Gamble, Gillette and AT&T. He has written and lectured extensively on the subject of brands, corporate identity, naming and brand valuation, and has been featured in numerous publications.

brand design for
digital viewing

A majority of people have a misconception regarding brands on the Internet – that they are different from other brands that have existed for decades. A brand is essentially a promise of an experience. It is a set of tangible and intangible elements which in tandem create an experience, or the promise of that experience, in someone's mind. So whether a brand is offered in a 12 oz. bottle, operates with an engine and a steering wheel, or is experienced only on the Internet, theoretically it's the same thing. The difference lies in the medium itself and the opportunities that the Internet provides to create a much more interpersonal brand relationship.

Virtually all of the world's leading brands have now embraced the Internet as an important communications vehicle. Today we see an online emporium of branded goods marketing themselves over the web – some like Amazon.com which were born as part of the Internet revolution – to more "traditional brands" such as GE who are using the Internet to create a more efficient learning and purchasing tool. Either way, brands now have the opportunity – or necessity – to create a unique interactive experience with their various constituencies. Those that do will create enormous wealth for their companies. Those that fail will most likely be relegated to the trivial pursuits of brand history.

> *"Companies that recognize the importance of their brand providing a road map for customers to help them navigate the increasingly complex waters will stand a better chance of success than the brands that are still shouting for recognition."*

These are enormously important waters for brand owners to navigate as brands today constitute significant value. In the days of yesteryear, wealth was measured by land – the more land you owned, the richer you were. People fought wars for land (and unfortunately still do today). As time moved on, we entered the Industrial Revolution, where wealth was judged not only by land, but by other tangible assets as well. Hard assets such as factories, printing presses, bottling plants and so forth were all indicators of corporate wealth. Today, we have entered an age where wealth is measured much less by tangible assets, but rather by intangible assets such as brands, copyrights, patents, formulae, and so on. One need only look at the stock market capitalization of leading companies, and the growing level of intangible assets which make up this total, to understand the significance of this changing dynamic. This is why the issue of brand development has moved beyond the marketing department into corporate boardrooms. It also underscores why the ability to build brands through the Internet has become more than just an exercise in HTML programming.

As with most new technologies there are a number of phases which constitute the growth cycle of their development. It's fairly obvious that the Internet is still in its infancy and therefore any real understanding of its scale is years away. However, we seem to have transitioned beyond the first phase of marketing goods over the Internet, and the "web-hype" which accompanied everything marketed over this new medium has begun to level itself out. In other words, we've seen the hysteria, the rush to get online, and the inevitable collapse of a multitude of new e-business ventures.

Much of this collapse can be attributed to a mistaken premise that great brands can be built by name recognition alone. Who can forget the 2000 US Super Bowl with the bombardment of 20 or so different ads from 20 or so new dot.com companies? Beyond the belief of these marketers – no doubt bolstered by venture capital funding – that they needed to "get their name out there," the true message of what they offered was lost. This is because name recognition on its own cannot replace the need for a brand to communicate a relevancy to key audiences. Those brands that understand this, create a unique and lasting bond with their audiences. Those who don't, find themselves shouting into an echo canyon simultaneously with hundreds of other brands. With the noise meter of our society already at deafening levels, it is practically impossible to remember or even care about these brands.

Our biggest challenge, therefore, is not just to gain name recognition for brands, but to create a relevance in a world where brands need to meet individual needs. We're entering an era where technology continues to shape our world and our daily lives. The power of what we will see tomorrow is far beyond what we can fathom today and the effect of this technological revolution will leave virtually no stone unturned. Medicine and transportation and a whole host of different industries will either be completely revitalized, reengineered, or become obsolete in the future because of what technology will create. And the companies that are able to adapt to the technology and think more for the future will have a greater chance of success. On that score, the companies that recognize the importance of their brand providing a road map for customers, to help them navigate the increasingly complex waters, will stand a better chance of success than the brands that are still shouting for recognition.

The question that all brands – online or offline – need to answer is, "How can you do something for me that provides value and is relevant to my needs?" The answer lies in coming up with a message that is useful and relevant to me as an individual. Conceptually, this is the same whether it be a brand of detergent or an online music store. However, the Internet allows the opportunity to create a more customized brand relationship than through traditional media. Through the Internet, I can tailor my messages to you. I can reach you in places I know you'll be. I can use data to understand what your individual preferences are. I can understand the kind of books you might like to read, the kind of music you might want to hear, and I can craft my message to you in a way that is much more personal and, therefore, much more relevant. And I can make this a two-way street allowing you to respond *back* to the brand in ways never before possible.

One of the most powerful tools to help create brand relevance is design. This is nothing new or surprising. The role of design has been universally recognized for years as a significant contributor to a brand's essence and personality. Many of today's leading brands, such as Shell and Nike, are known as much for their graphic symbols as their typefaces. Brands like Apple have reinvigorated their very existence through revolutionary product design. And stores such as French-based Sephora have demonstrated how environmental design can create a unique in-store brand experience and enhanced sales.

The design of web-based applications is no less important than other forms of brand design and will play an even greater role in brand building in the future. What began as the translation of written brochures into HTML-based 'webzines,' the design of brand websites has developed in parallel with advancing technologies to create more sophisticated user interfaces and engaging user experiences. These technologies are allowing us new design opportunities while also testing old paradigms regarding brand identity as a static two-dimensional experience.

This doesn't mean necessarily that the basic elements of a brand's identity will need to change on the web, but the manner in which this identity is communicated will most likely change often. This is possibly due to technologies which allow us to dimensionalize the brand further than traditional media has previously allowed. For example, rather than seeing an automotive advertisement in a magazine, we can now transport ourselves *virtually* into the "local" dealership, look around, get inside a particular vehicle and get a feel for the interior. On some sites we can even negotiate to buy the car online. Who knows? Perhaps in the future we'll be able to take a test drive as well. This is a different brand experience than what we can create in other media and therefore creates a more expansive opportunity to build brand relevance.

However, this relevance will need to be created in conjunction with the technology it is built on. While the computer has long provided opportunities to create design that is more innovative and precise, today's technologies are pushing us to design multisensory experiences which go far beyond the origins of graphic design. For example, it was only 15–20 years ago when designs were expressed mostly by hand. A graphic designer would typically sketch conceptual elements by hand, and present many different sketches as graphic solutions. In the mid-1980s, the design industry was revolutionized by computer-aided design which created time efficiencies by eliminating lengthy refinements. This created opportunities to express new ideas more quickly and has become the standard for what is today's graphic design business. In fact, most young designers today are not illustrators, but rather computer designers whose talents are more associated with software literacy than with hand artistry. Nevertheless, these are the designers of the present and undoubtedly the future, whose ideas are expressed as well (or even better!) by their mastery of such software as Quark and Illustrator, as well as newer HTML-based versions such as Flash and Alias.

While the tools are different, the design process itself has stayed the same and will do so indefinitely. This holds true in all facets of design whether one is designing a new logo, the interior of a bank, or a new website. It always begins with a brand idea which provides the platform on which the brand should be communicated to its key audiences. However, in web-based applications we have new tools available to us to express this idea. Our designers are continually being trained and retrained in web-based software which will create new avenues and opportunities for web design. Not only must we be cognizant of these new technologies and be capable of designing within their specifications, we must also remember that technology should be an enabler and therefore not encumber our impression of the site or its navigation effectiveness.

There are essentially three main components to designing a successful website. First and foremost, is the site's ability to communicate successfully the brand message and idea. Unfortunately, we see many examples of web-based design which have focused more on the technology and less on the message. While the idea of having flying cows on the screen, or overlaying loud firecracker sounds may be fun for the designers, it most likely has nothing to do with establishing a brand relevance with users. I once heard Michael Eisner mention that all new initiatives in the Magic Kingdom should be "Disney-like" (and profitable). No matter how "cool" a specific attraction might be, if it does not fit the Disney brand values and message it is not to be considered. The same principle holds true for a brand website. All elements of the site – both technically and graphically – must be in line with the brand idea or should not be utilized.

The second characteristic of design success is the ease of navigation employed by the site. As many sites are designed without understanding the true needs of the consumer, we often find ourselves in an online version of

Houdini's Great Escape, trying to navigate through unnecessary clutter and "brandstanding" of the company or product. Keep the navigation map as simple and easy to understand as possible. Creating a site with multiple click through may not sound like a big deal, but fails to appreciate that, while you have the interest level to navigate your own site, others generally do not.

The last component in designing a successful website is creating the flexibility to keep the brand fresh and relevant. Like other media outlets, brands need to adapt new and relevant messages on an ongoing basis in order to stay current. Even the most tried and true advertising campaigns eventually get a makeover or a variation of the theme. The message and design of a brand website is no different. It requires a flexible format to allow ongoing changes to occur without bearing the cost or time of redesigning the entire site.

This flexibility is also important because of the rapid level of change which is happening all around us. The advent of the microprocessor has changed our society faster in the past 10 years than in perhaps the past 50. These changes have created a proliferation of brands which has required brand owners to focus their efforts more attentively on establishing and maintaining key brand equities. And yet, we must ensure that the balancing act of maintaining brand equity is not overshadowed by the need to adapt certain modifications to the brand which keep it fresh and more relevant to today's consumer.

The good news is that digital media allows us the ability to change much faster than we've ever done before. And platforms such as the web provide the opportunity to change the expression of a brand over and over again at a relatively low cost. This doesn't advocate that we should change the Hertz rental car brand color from yellow to green. But it does suggest that Hertz can create new buying opportunities by continually redesigning its site to better maximize new technologies and customer expectations. Equally, the brand should make it as easy to transact with "online" as it would be "off line."

Thus, you should be able to do all your ticketing and transactions with the company over the web, enhancing your relationship with the Hertz brand. This is really what the Internet is offering: a two-way relationship based on the customer's specific needs.

The online experience also gives marketers the opportunity to dimensionalize their brand. We can use three-dimensional applications and expressions of the brand through new software and new technologies that did not exist before. One of the biggest advantages is our ability to create an interactive experience to build the brand relationship. Consumers have been bombarded by communications from brands that told us why they are the best, or taste the best, or look the best, or clean our clothes better than the others. Today, we the consumers are able to write in and talk to owners or stewards of the brand about the brand's efficacy, and comment in real time about our experience with brands. This interaction (and feedback) goes a long way in building a relationship with the consumer and cementing brand loyalty.

These design opportunities are particularly interesting for the more established product categories like packaged goods. In this capacity we can create different experiences online than you would have in the supermarket or at the store shelf. We can communicate in a much more individualized manner, and communicate directly to our target audience. An example is the IAMS brand of pet food. In the site for IAMS, we can learn about cats and dogs in a way which provides valuable information about their diets and raising home pets. There is also a chat forum from which to learn about other pet owners' experiences and to ask questions about your own pet. This type of site creates a pact with the consumer that extends beyond what is inside a can of dog food and bestows an authoritative position for the brand. And it can do this on a global basis as well, with very little cost variation to the original site.

Along with the possibilities for developing a stronger brand presence through the web, our expectations of the online experience have increased exponentially. While many people seem to have moved beyond general concerns over credit card security, the ability of a brand to transact over the web places a new burden on the provision of customer service and brand image in general. In other words, brand attributes are manifest not only in the product itself, but also in other aspects of the experience. For example, if I buy a new video on Amazon.com, my assumption is that I will experience the Amazon brand through the attributes of the video I've purchased – does it work properly, is the format compatible, and so on. Additionally, I am experiencing the Amazon brand through the personalized service and after-sale experience. It must fulfill its promise by delivering the video to me in two days to the right address and for the price that was quoted. All of these elements therefore contribute to the online experience and must be consistent with all other elements of design and communications.

We've had an onslaught of new brands into the global market very quickly, because the Internet is a low-cost vehicle for creating and launching new brands. Companies would have had to spend hundreds of millions of dollars to create the same level of awareness and exposure as today's Internet enables. In our world today, we face sensory overload in all aspects of our life. We are bombarded by dozens of messages that hit our brain before we even get to work in the morning. There's no possible way that we can take all of that in. While new brands gain an advantage by entering the market more quickly through the Internet, the consumer is faced with increasingly more choices. Using the Internet to build or extend a brand will help to alleviate the confusion. Companies that understand that using the Internet to communicate their brand's point of view, their vision of the world, will be able to connect with their constituencies in a relevant way.

As we peer into the future, I believe brand design will undergo a great many changes. There will continue to be a growing influence in the area of product design. The form and the shape of the product itself will move more to the forefront to differentiate one brand from another. The Internet, too, will dictate, along with the technologies that become available, a more multisensory brand experience, and one that is more three dimensional. We will expect to be behind the wheel of the car online. We will expect to take a virtual tour of the house from the real estate agent and the hotel before we embark on our travel. The brand design we undertake over the Internet will require a rich tapestry of multimedia, greater use of three-dimensional applications, and more interactive feedback mechanisms. These designs will need to become more global as there is no such thing as a local brand on the Internet. Brand design therefore will need to express the essence of the brand on a global basis, meaning less variation in design worldwide.

I think the designer of the future will have to be much more holistic in the way he or she thinks about brand design than they have been in the past. Even today, in a company such as Interbrand, we have design groups that specialize in packaged goods or retail environments or corporate graphics or the Internet. The designer of the future will have to think more about how these disciplines work together. I think that as fast as the world is moving now, it will be twice as fast ten years from now. Designers will be relying on more sophisticated software and technologies to do their job more efficiently. Tomorrow's brand designs will be researched both online and offline, and will convey information through a host of web appliances. Brands will have more opportunities to form partnerships to showcase their offerings of interest to their audiences, and streaming media will help brands to define their personalities.

We will need to utilize a host of other communications media to help to create a more holistic expression of the brand in the marketplace. An online presence is a very powerful tool by which to communicate a brand's essence. Television and print are also important media, and, coupled with an online presence, you can make a very powerful statement about your brand. We see opportunities that exist through the web which are different from the opportunities that exist in television, broadcast and print. In the main, however, they all work together, or should work together, to create a singular message in the marketplace. The genesis of what constitutes powerful brands in the future will include those that work both offline and online seamlessly.

In fact, I do not think that in the future we will be talking about *online* brands versus *offline* brands. Nor do I not think we'll be writing books about 'e-brands' in ten years time because the web will not be defined that way. Essentially, a brand is a brand is a brand. It will be no different from saying that because you have a strong presence through television advertising that we will call this a t-brand or that your satellite advertising will make you an s-brand. You are only an e-brand today because the technology is new. In the future, we will be looking at it much more holistically. We will be looking to create a singular brand experience that uses a variety of different vehicles, with the Internet as one of those communication vehicles. We're already starting to see it that way. The rush by brand manufacturers to get online has subsided. The brand companies are moving to very interesting ways of communicating with their audience and moving away from just crafting new websites. So, in the future, brands online and offline will be part of our everyday life.

There is a joke going around that in ten years time there will be only five companies, because everybody will merge with everybody else. Then all the companies will start breaking each other up once more into smaller companies as part of a new competitive strategy. This back and forth view of corporate development is somewhat analogous to the future development of the Internet and the advent of website design. Sooner or later those brands who have entered our world as part of the digital revolution – and those who have reengineered themselves to take advantage of this media – will need to embrace the web not just as a mechanism for gaining size, but also as an opportunity to establish a new brand experience with their constituencies.

It is much easier for a company to enter markets more quickly than ever before. Brands will have to be able to compete on a global scale with their design reflecting the global nature of their business. But bigger is not always better. A brand must be relevant to its consumer in order to survive. And it is the brand's relevance that will keep a brand strong and vital.

rudynadilo

Rudy Nadilo

President and Chief Executive Officer

greenfieldonline

Rudy Nadilo joined Greenfield Online, Inc. in 1997 as its first President and CEO. The company is the pioneer and leading provider of marketing research using the Internet. He is a recognized expert in online marketing research, consumer panel behavioral information, database marketing, the use of retail scanner information to support the marketing services industry, and the application of computer technology in these fields. Prior to joining Greenfield Online, Nadilo was the Senior Vice President of Marketing of Information Resources, Inc., and he has held management positions at Dancer Fitzgerald Sample Advertising, Richardson Vicks and J. Walter Thompson Advertising.

8 interactive brand design research

"Get a website, put it up, people will come and buy your product," is what people used to say a few years ago. Along with that simplified notion came the notion that perhaps there's a real difference between an e-brand and an offline brand. There is no real difference. A brand is still a brand. The Internet certainly gives you another means to build the brand, but it is important to understand the different elements of marketing on the Internet and the different channels you have to help support that brand. The online brand has to be treated with great care and support, because online loyalty can be lost at the click of a mouse.

It was also thought that the only way to market an e-brand was online. But more and more, we're finding that online brands need the help of offline marketing and offline brands need online marketing.

There probably was a time when you could easily differentiate between e-brands and traditional brands. For example, Amazon was an e-brand, and

Abercrombie was a traditional brand. Now, that doesn't seem to be the case. Amazon is all over the media with outdoor print and TV advertising – and Abercrombie is online.

> *"With the notion of a dynamic tracking study, you can have your own users and your competitors' users, and tap into that study at any given point in time."*

Jim McCann, from 1-800 Flowers, summed it up beautifully. He said that your brand has to be 360 degrees today. Your online has to complement your offline, which has to complement your print, which has to complement this and that, and if you're not looking at the consumer in every direction, you can lose.

Yet, a year ago, if somebody said, "1-800 Flowers.com," the Silicon Valley crowd would go, "Ugh, what a bunch of idiots. They don't get it." Well, guess what? Jim McCann not only got it, he eclipsed everyone. So, the mentality has shifted to a point where e-branding has to be part of the total branding strategy and total marketing strategy. Any place that's not just a candy store on the corner will need to be online.

The shift to online branding gives the consumer more control than ever before. When you look at the chat rooms and bulletin boards, you get the feeling that a brand could be made or broken in a matter of hours. We've seen that sort of thing in the offline world as well, where the media has strong control over the success or failure of a brand. Online, every consumer has this control.

Basically, chat rooms can be grudge rooms where people who have complaints against a specific company or product go and take over the chat room, fomenting a mini-revolution. So, a brand that doesn't already have a strong foundation can be destroyed because of the power of communication on the Internet.

Online research has changed the scope of gathering information. For a researcher, this is very exciting. If you look at the methodologies we had available to us to collect the information – the continuum from door-to-door to malls, telephones and mail – each had its limitations. Of course, online has limitations too, but it opens up an entirely new way of doing research. It's not as time consuming. There's immediacy to it, and it's totally anonymous. We find that people will talk to us about the most sensitive topics imaginable, people feel safe on the web. It has the immediacy and the intimacy of email. The respondents feel comfortable. They do it on their time and they're not put off by interruptions at inconvenient times. It's totally revolutionized the way data can be collected. Since the web is based on a feeling of community, respondents are comfortable as a part of our online research community.

For example, we did a study for a long-established personal care products manufacturer on shaving practices among men and women. One might think that such a company would know everything there is to know about shaving. Yet the descriptions from respondents were so graphic in nature and revealed such personal information that they had to be edited before being presented to management, who were just amazed when they read them. It took online research to deliver these insights into how their product was being used.

Online research works for brands and products that change quickly. We're doing studies that are a lot timelier. Clients can make quicker decisions when the research follows right along with what the respondents are doing. Some of the clients that we work with have had four generations of evolvement in two years with the new economy. They change on the run and keep moving. Other clients want to know whether they should take their brand to the web, go wireless, or take their brand into new areas. Online research is guiding their decisions.

It's great to understand online technology, but we attribute our success to also understanding business and realizing that successful online brands require much more than technology. When you look at the e-brands, there is a lot of pollution out there, and many are disappearing because they thought technology alone would keep them going.

We even said two years ago that our name Greenfield Online could come back to bite us. The word "online" is itself limiting in terms of potential. We are a research company utilizing the latest in technology. We want to use leading edge technology incorporating state-of-the-art communications to collect both research and information, and to allow clients ultimately to make smarter marketing decisions. That's our vision. When we talk about state-of-the-art technology, we mean everything that's out there, not just online. We also know that new methodologies such as wireless will keep changing, so we have to be prepared to change with them.

One of our clients wanted to stay in touch with farmers, so we used our QuickTake™ research product and incorporated two-way pagers in order to give and get weather reports, crop price information and so on. Once a week, the pagers go off with questions for the farmers who answer them right on the spot, even while they're on their tractors. So, we have a content partner with agricultural information of value to every farmer, and every day they can get information on whatever they want – grain prices, weather or whatever. This is all being done through a terminal. When the client pushes the "submit" button, the questions go out to the pagers through a wireless system. The farmers answer on their pagers, and the answers come back into the terminal. This information comes in from hundreds of people and gets reduced to one single chart, graph, or whatever is needed to best communicate the results. It's terrific. Wireless technology is now reaching an audience that was usually only reached by phone late at night, and rarely reached at all during growing or harvest season. So now you don't have to actually send people out into the field, find the farmers on their tractors as they're working, or talk to them and write down the answers. The totally wireless technology is with them wherever they are – in the middle of the field or taking a break. These farmers also have the great advantage of getting the information they need right away.

Think for a moment about this notion of an information ASP. Our vision is that, soon, a majority of our products and services will be relayed online, instead of having to rely on receiving the final information through hard copies and PowerPoint presentations. Added value to clients will be that the clients will be able to do their own cross-tabbing, look up information, have the results of studies and be able to get answers to their questions right away. With focus groups online, nobody has to travel or eat the bad food in the focus group facility. Now you can be at home at your own computer, at the office or in a hotel with your laptop following the focus group activity. Clients can get the information they need wherever they are.

One of our client companies, who makes a computer peripheral, gets information on product usage directly online. They no longer have to worry about managing a twenty thousand person user panel to get this kind of information. Through custom online research, they can identify exactly what their customers are doing with their products. The software for this application is built into customers' computers and monitors product usage. As researchers, we know how to take their information and tie it back into our clients' population database of consumer information. We help them to profile the way consumers use their products so that they can plan for the future.

Think of the capabilities that are available through tracking online. There will be more real-time information in the future. Product managers will arrive in the morning, and check their in-use study from the night before, or get relatively instant information about the progress of a campaign. They can put a new package on the shelf and not only know how it's moving, but also have people pushing buttons somewhere to tell us how they like the brand and the product. That's not far off.

The brand managers at a major food company can have an ongoing set of consumers and an ongoing log of information through our company. We can set up these ongoing logs and give them tools such as QuickTake™, which open dialogues with their consumers. They can get this key information on a daily basis. They see certain buying indicators in the morning and look in the afternoon to see other buying indicators. The large sales force can be in constant communication with the head office. This communication can go on 24 hours a day, 52 weeks a year. The soft drink salesperson who goes into a store in Tulsa and sees some strange brand can go back to his hotel that night, log on, and be communicating with the other company salespersons from all over the country. All of a sudden, competitive intelligence has become a key weapon for large sales forces. This is where research will be used. It will greatly impact marketing strategies because it provides instanta-neous intelligence. With this real-time feedback, anyone who has a valuable brand would be remiss not to take advantage of it. Using this information correctly enables one to build a brand more quickly and more successfully.

Without spending a fortune, companies can now maintain an ongoing dynamic panel of people with literally thousands of ongoing responses, and have the tools at their desk to get any answer they want whenever they want it.

Our product, called MindStorm™, is geared for online research. It is comparable to having a focus group that can last for a week, or even longer. It goes on 24 hours a day, 7 days a week. People log on any time they want during the period. For instance, if the research were on a new product idea, participants would go through the process of deciding how they want to interact with the product, what they'd do with it and so forth. Designers can have respondents look at a package design on a Monday, then tweak it, and on Wednesday show them a new one based on what they said on Monday. This can go on for as long as you want, and with the same people.

With broadband, there will be more developed systems for researching such things as packaging. Right now, we can take a design, put it in a j-peg file, get the three-dimensional modeling, attach it to a questionnaire, press a button and send it overnight to a couple of hundred people. The people see it from all sides and answer some questions. The next morning you get a read on how your consumers like your new package design.

Online enables research to become personalized. Amazon sent out a personalized note that I got today from Jeff Bezos. Obviously, it's not really from him. He probably sent it out to a million customers. But it's three things: one, a research study; two, a direct mail piece and three, it's a great CRM piece because he's asking my opinion before he makes a change to the website. It makes me feel like I'm connected with a brand. The future will see more stuff like that where the consumer participates with the brand.

What Jeff Bezos has accomplished is brilliant. It's as though he said to his customers, "We've made a new design, we've changed our package, but before we go out with it, we want you, our valued customer, to see it first and let us know if there's anything you don't like about it." That connects you to the brand and to the process, and it's building a new community. It's being part of the Amazon community where you get emails every week telling you what's new in the category you're interested in. If you're a history buff, you get email every week with the new history book of the week.

There is that fine line, though, that you can't cross in terms of one-on-one marketing. You've got to be careful to avoid blending research and promotion. It would be unacceptable to ask whether people like A or B and then in two weeks, send all the people who picked B a special B promotion. Our research has to aggregate. We cannot go back to a company and say here are the names of specific people who are most likely to buy your product. This would deteriorate the value of getting objective third party information and it's where data mining, marketing and research still have some barriers.

We see Greenfield Online as a brand on the Internet. When you think of Greenfield Online, we want you to think of trust, loyalty and someone to whom you could give information, and someone who will use that information professionally. If we ever were seen to be giving away personal information on people, it would hurt our brand. So there must be some real fundamentals in terms of privacy.

Some of the things that are scary about research privacy involve the possibility of chips smaller than the size of your watch that send out information based on where you are. If I'm driving by a Wal-Mart, I can get notified that Wal-Mart is up the street and has a special deal on certain items. Of course this isn't the type of research that we would do, but there are applications coming that could become effective through these technologies.

Another thing we should be careful about is sending out commercial messages when seeking answers. The Internet is a free zone, but I don't want a commercial message if I don't ask for it. Casual messages are OK, but it's inappropriate to promote products through emails using the premise of research. There's an enormous amount of passion out there about the right way to market brands and products online. So Greenfield Online is cautious about its relationship with respondents. Within our Greenfield Online community, you first have to click on something that says, "Share your opinion", in order to join. Then you come to our site. You fill out a form at our site, which clearly tells you why you're filling it out, to share your opinions and research. Then you get an email back thanking you for filling out the form and confirming you've done this. It gives you an opportunity to drop out. So, by the time you're in, you know it isn't for promotion. We have a Digital Consumer Bill of Rights there to show people that nothing will be used for promotional purposes. We've taken a hard stance on privacy from day one. We make sure people understand what we're going to do with their information, so that there's no question. Brands and companies don't want to wind up with hundreds of daily emails from people requesting to be removed from their list.

We also make sure that people understand that if we ask them personal questions, we use it for an aggregate of answers, not personal information.

People used to say, "You'll never get information this way. People are going to freeze up." Well, we go through thousands of surveys a day with people willingly giving us personal information. They know exactly what we're going to do with that information and how it's going to be used.

A lot of research in the future will be more passive than active. With fifty thousand people in a panel that has a GPS locator chip, there will be information that people will have right away. Can you imagine tracking someone down to an aisle of a grocery store and being able to tell which aisle the people skip over or which aisle they stop at?

Consider what scanners did for passive information. They blew out the old way of counting items sold. Passive information will grow, but custom research will not go away either. Combining the two, with the technology that now allows you to do it, is key. You can infer buying patterns through the passive method and get explicit answers through other research.

One thing that you might have seen lately is the radio UPC codes that will be on packages from the store. A consumer can pick up the packages, fill up the cart and walk right out the door, because each package will emit a signal regarding its cost, and the consumer will be charged automatically.

When is offline appropriate and when is online appropriate for research? Our estimates show that online research in the next five years will account for 40% of total research revenues. Others predict that online will be 75–80% by then. We disagree. It's just physically impossible. We'll still need scanner tracking, audits and surveys. Offline focus groups will still be done, mall intercepts and in-home product placements will still be with us.

Even with package design, we can show it on the Internet, turn it and even show the inside of the package but we can't fill it up online. We can't have people hold it and see how it feels with hot coffee in it.

Remember, that for many of the things that have to do with the brand, we will still need offline research. We all know how in taste-tests, sometimes the brand overwhelms the taste. Where there's anything tactile associated with the brand, there will certainly be limitations on conducting the online research.

We did a study on what people look for in online customer support, even thinking that the email or live chat would be the number one thing. Well, at this point, the number one thing for customer support is the 800 number.

On the flip side, there are things that you can do online that you just can't do offline. Look at the time you can save with models of products that can be designed, engineered, and shown online. This can save package goods companies millions of dollars, especially by showing it on the Internet rather than bringing people into a room to talk about it. With our QuickTake™ technology, companies can put together their own surveys, and get answers very quickly. They can put in their password, and build a survey. It's perfect for PR firms. Think of getting a quick read on what was happening after something about your company appeared on the news. A PR person could just build a survey and get answers very quickly online.

Online research in the future will be more integrated with marketing strategy in general. Packaged goods companies have often embraced research as part of their marketing strategy, and are in the infant stages of embracing it online. Financial institutions have been strong with research. But we are finding that many technology companies don't understand what marketing research is used for. They still think they can do two focus groups and then launch a product. Take the Apple Newton, which was a brilliant product. Perhaps it was pushed out too soon, but, in its third generation, the Newton had handwriting recognition down cold. You could give it to a doctor and it would recognize the writing. It was great. But Apple, who spends millions of dollars on great design, never fully researched the customers that used the Newton. They didn't know that their users didn't really want just a stand-alone, handheld product. Then take the folks at Palm. They introduced a simple thing and what does it do? It does what the users want – it syncs with their computer. Now how did they figure that out? They talked to people. Apple did not do their homework with their customers and Palm did. So, the research industry has a lot of potential in terms of recruiting technology companies. With the notion of a dynamic tracking study, you can have your own users and your competitors' users and tap into that at any given point in time. And the smart marketers will see the advantages in that and will start doing that.

We also have to keep in mind that computing will be different several years from now. The Internet will go where you need it to be, and the term online will disappear completely. It will be taken for granted. When I say I'm going to call you later, it might not be a cell phone or a cordless phone or whatever phone. It will mean I'm going to communicate with you. We know how wireless is changing the way people communicate, and through wireless I can check emails, stock quotes and sport scores. That's why companies such as Amazon and eBay are rushing into that market – so they can watch their customers. If the research companies are not out there and their panels are not moved to the next wave of technology, they will lose out. Even now, the Greenfield panel can be used through a wireless device.

New economy branding is starting to extend really quickly beyond the computer on your desk and it's coming from many different directions.

I don't watch TV the same way I used to since I now have Tivo, the interactive TV service. This is very interesting because our company is working on using these approaches to do our research. Many companies, so far, have bought into Tivo channels. I can go to one network and see the feature movies that they have to offer. This is another way of the network putting itself in front of the person. Networks are adding channels and categories, and all these channels and categories will be branded. Networks such as NBC and others are buying Internet companies and trying to figure out the best way to use them. Disney is buying companies one after another. These networks will show the same faces that you see online. Many have tied in very well with other companies to make sure that they're constantly in front of the consumer.

If I were a TV advertiser, I'd be pretty nervous right now because they're the ones that will get stuck changing their channels. The concept of a 30-second commercial might be extinct ten years from now. There was a successful episode of *Friends* on TV where the merchandiser at Pottery Barn ran an experiment. The "Friends" got the Pottery Barn catalog and everything that was in their apartment was Pottery Barn merchandise. The episode played the night before the catalog was shipped out. So Pottery Barn was able to correlate the TV show to the sales. This is how advertising can change. You can be watching a show, and if you like a product you see, click on it. This will take you to the product website where you can buy it. That's a very powerful thing coming our way. We have to make sure that research is one step ahead of all of this. If the device of the future is a combination of cell phone, organizer, Internet portal and TV, all in one, we'll be there.

When you think about the branding and the design, the exciting thing is that the revolution has just begun. There are probably fifteen more places that your brand will have to exist in the next ten years for communicating to the audience, and you'll have to adapt to it. Research will help to solve the problem of what the consumer wants and needs, and that's why research is critically important to the marketer in the process. With research, we get the information to help marketers to make these changes.

Telecommunication companies are required to exist in all these different spaces and what they're going to find out is that they won't be able to just peel off their logo and stick it on the web. They will have to reinvent themselves as they go. Online research will be there for them and for other industries like them, and I think that will be great fun for all of us.

daveburwick

David A. Burwick
Senior Vice President, Marketing
Carbonated Soft Drinks
pepsi-colanorthamerica

Dave Burwick is responsible for the marketing and advertising of Pepsi's entire car-
bonated soft drink business, representing nearly 90% of the volume and profit for
Pepsi-Cola North America. Brands include Pepsi, Diet Pepsi, Pepsi ONE, Wild Cherry
Pepsi, Mountain Dew, Mug, Sierra Mist, Slice and all line extensions. Since joining
Pepsi in 1989, Burwick has been involved in several brand marketing positions. Most
recently, he was Vice President, Marketplace Initiative Development, where he over-
saw Pepsi's consumer promotions, sports marketing, grassroots marketing and
Internet marketing. He also served as Vice President of Flavors, Director of Mountain
Dew, Director of Core Events, and Mountain Dew Brand Manager. He was instrumen-
tal in building Mountain Dew into the fastest growing soft drink of the 1990s.

9 interfacing with the consumer

Today, anytime you talk about marketing in the future, it's about marketing on
the Internet. It's a moving target. What's new today will be entirely different
next year. That applies to Pepsi as much as to any other consumer products
company. But, for a product category such as carbonated soft drinks, with
its overwhelmingly young consumer profile, it is perhaps even more critical
to know how to use the Internet effectively.

Our marketing department is divided into two groups: carbonated and non-
carbonated beverages. The carbonated group includes Pepsi, Diet Pepsi,
Pepsi ONE, Mountain Dew, Sierra Mist, and so on – anything with bubbles.
The non-carbonated group includes brands such as Aquafina (water),
FruitWorks (juice) and our joint ventures with Lipton and Starbucks. This
group is also working with our sister company – Tropicana – to launch its
Dole brand in single-serve bottles for convenience stores.

The group that I am heading – carbonated soft drinks – is brand new. We created it about two years ago to combine the efforts that once cut across brands, such as consumer promotions, sports marketing and grassroots marketing. But, as each brand group's responsibilities had become very broad and they did not have the ability to go deep in any area, we decided to keep the advertising, brand strategy, and broad business-building initiatives within each brand team and place other responsibilities elsewhere.

"There are many ways to promote your products effectively on the Internet. But first we need to break out of this mindset that broadcast advertising – specifically TV advertising – is the only way to do this."

Many of these "other responsibilities" are handled by a group called Marketplace Initiative Development (MID). There are two other groups within MID – one that handles consumer promotions and another that produces customer-selling materials. This includes a sports marketing team so that, for the first time, we have seven or eight people solely dedicated to building brands and driving volume through sports – whether it be Major League Baseball, Major League Soccer, Jeff Gordon, or our relationship with ESPN and the X Games. We also have developed an Internet team. For the last six months or so, I've been involved with our Internet strategy because it cuts across all our brands.

There's also a group called Marketing Services that works with all our suppliers to contract for point-of-purchase materials, premiums and things of that nature. This group includes a pretty significant in-house design team, with several permanent art directors, that does the development work for a lot of basic POP and package design. In addition, we also use a number of freelancers.

Occasionally, for a project such as Mountain Dew packaging, we bring in several design firms to handle different phases. For any given assignment, we might bring in four or five different design firms for a burst of energy and creativity. If one of these does an especially good job, we might keep going with that group until the project is completed.

As for e-branding, we are running an online/offline promotion with Yahoo! called PepsiStuff.com, and it's fantastic. What we have done historically for Pepsi – as an e-brand, if you will – has really been through the Pepsi web site, www.pepsi.com. We call this PepsiWorld. We built the site in 1996, long before many other brands or companies did this kind of promotion. Visitors can really get a sense of what the brand is all about – from entertainment to music and sports. We try to integrate this with our Pepsi advertising – whether it's Faith Hill or KISS or Jeff Gordon – so when you go and experience PepsiWorld, you can experience many of the key equities of the Pepsi brand. One way is through our KISS webcast, which allows visitors to see and hear a KISS concert right on our site.

This year, the amount of people that have visited PepsiWorld has increased dramatically. We're now up to almost three million people a month, which is huge for a branded site. We don't think there's another site in the consumer packaged goods business that gets as many hits as we do per month. We change the PepsiWorld program every month. It's fun. And, in this way, we communicate it in our advertising, on our packaging and on our POP materials, so people know where to find us.

In the past, we had a "build it and they will come" mentality. Early on, that made sense, but we've learned that – no matter how much we hate to admit it – there's no reason that consumers *have to* go to PepsiWorld. There are a lot of sites that have great content, such as ESPN and Yahoo! Inherently, PepsiWorld, a manufacturer-based site, is not necessarily a favorite online destination. We will continue to evolve the Pepsi sites so that they serve as a home base for consumers to go to find out more about our company and our products.

Our Internet partner, Yahoo!, has 120 million registered users to our three million. We'd be foolish to think that activity on our sites will attract and reach all the people we want to reach. This is what drew us to Yahoo! and led us to develop a partnership with them. We think Yahoo! is the hottest and most highly regarded brand on the web. Their attitude is very youthful, progressive and optimistic – just like the Pepsi brand – and so we believe it's a really good match for us.

Brand Pepsi has a very broad target but our primary target is under thirty. The wave of the future for getting or keeping teens and young adults on our site is by providing entertainment value. It's really using the medium for what it does best: engaging and entertaining people.

But we are also cautious as we recognize that our co-competency as a company is not just providing entertainment online, but advertising our products. Certainly, from an advertising perspective, we perceive Pepsi advertising and Mountain Dew advertising as Hollywood-style entertainment and we try and bring that same value online. But we also know that there are a lot of other places where people can go online to get similar value.

That's why we don't want to stop there. What we want to do is be where our consumers are and one of those places is the Internet. Consumers are spending less time watching TV and more time online – there is a direct correlation. If we want to continue to be relevant to our consumers, we need to be an integral part of their lives. If their lives are going to a baseball game, we want to be there. If they are watching MTV or ESPN, we need to be there also. And if they are going online to Yahoo!, we need to be there as well. The idea isn't to replace any TV advertising, the idea is to be where our consumers are. If they are in front of the TV we need to be there, and if they're on the Internet we have to be there also.

But there is a big difference between the two. The Internet is interactive by its nature and its activities and engagements are constantly changing. Going online is a much more active experience, so you need to provide people with an opportunity to be active and use the Internet the way it was meant to be used. Watching TV is a passive experience. For that reason, you cannot have the same type of advertising or communication on TV as on the Internet. You need to leverage each medium for its strength.

A great example of this is our PepsiStuff.com program. It's amazing work. In the first 24 hours of the program, 18,000 people registered, and in the first two months, two million people registered. We did this program in the summer of 1996 and then again in the summer of 1997. Essentially, the way it worked is when consumers bought Pepsi or Mountain Dew, they earned points on the packaging. They cut out and saved points that they could use to order T-shirts, hats, gym bags, leather jackets, all sorts of apparel, from a nice, glossy catalog.

While this was hugely successful it was also hugely expensive for us to do. The fulfillment costs for this type of program were very high. We had to match the expected redemption with the inventories and manage those inventories very carefully. This was an extremely difficult thing to do.

But consumers loved the idea. They thought "Hey, Pepsi rewarded me for buying Pepsi." It's not a new idea. Certainly, S&H Green Stamps did continuity programs years ago. Marlboro Cigarettes took it to another level and we took it to another level again. We also brought some of the glitz that Pepsi had with it. All sorts of famous up-and-coming athletes, such as Jeff Gordon, Mia Hamm, Derek Jeter, Lisa Leslie and Deion Sanders, were part of the catalog. This was fun but, again, it was very expensive. Although we spent millions of dollars each year, we couldn't quite get the value right for the consumer and we couldn't afford to spend more.

That is what brings us to PepsiStuff.com. We have taken the program and basically moved it entirely online. Here's how it works. When you buy a 20-ounce or one-liter bottle of Pepsi or Mountain Dew – our primary packages for convenience stores and younger consumers – you twist off the cap and there's a 10-digit code under the cap. You go online to PepsiStuff.com, set up an account, enter the code and get the points. For every cap you enter you get 100 points. You can then redeem your points for prizes on the site.

We also have pulled in several Yahoo! shopping partners that are offering online discounts. One of them is Electronic Arts, a video game supplier for Nintendo and Sony PlayStation. Others are Sony Music, Sony Pictures and Sam Goody. As you go on buying Pepsi and saving points, there are literally tens of thousands of prizes for which you can exchange your points, such as Sony CDs, $2 off at SamGoody.com, or electronic music downloads. You also can bid on auction items.

You may ask where this is going in the future. The ability to integrate online and offline programs for consumers is exactly where we want to be. It's an offline program when you buy Pepsi or Mountain Dew in a convenience store. But once you have bought them and have collected these caps, you can go into the online world, the world of Pepsi Cola and Mountain Dew. Having partners further enhances our brands, because we're partnering with companies that deliver messages that are as strong on brand equity and imagery as ours. At the same time, we are driving value to consumers and we are driving volume. It's the first time we have actually been able to build brands and drive volume at the same time.

Yahoo! is a major partner and the beauty of it is how it works financially for us. Of course, we have to pay Yahoo! money to be advertised on Yahoo! But they handle all the site forms. We couldn't hire people that could develop the same sites. It's just too robust, too difficult. The Yahoo! folks are experts at building a site. Yahoo! builds the sites, and in addition, develops promotions on all our packaging – 1.5 billion packages. On all our packaging, we have a Yahoo! logo plus Sony, Electronic Arts and Sam Goody. Concurrently, it gives Yahoo! a chance to get 1.5 billion impressions in a channel that is new to them – convenience stores where 13–29 year-olds shop.

That's a perfect example of how a partnership between Pepsi and an online company can have huge reach. With almost a million points of distribution in this country, including about 120,000 convenience stores where we sell our products, we are bringing our partners into these convenience stores where they have no way of getting there on their own. In return, they are providing us with a lot of the prizes. Together, we're on the front page of the Yahoo! site where we are advertising this program. It is a fantastic partnership that really takes advantage of the online world and the power of reaching consumers and doing things that you can only do online.

We also tie into all our off-site promotions. Anytime we have a consumer promotion, you can go online to find out more about it. So, instead of having to look at the rules on a tear pad in a grocery store, or find out about the program by reading the fine print on the bottom of a twelve-pack wrap, you can go online.

Of course, a lot of consumer packaged goods companies do consumer in-store promotions, but it's so hard to communicate our full message to consumers when we are limited to the packaging. There is not a lot of room on the packages, or the tear sheets disappear and consumers lose interest in the program. If they know they can go online to find out about it, it's going to keep them involved and engaged in the program.

Several months before the launch of PepsiStuff.com, we ran a program where you could actually create your own CDs. This is another example of how to use the Internet. In this program, you bought Pepsi or Mountain Dew, collected points, sent them in and chose from a list of two hundred different songs from different Warner Music artists, everything from Kid Rock to Faith Hill. Depending on how many points you sent in, you could either get a five-track custom CD or an eleven-track custom CD.

The beauty of the Internet is that we could add artists as the program was developing and people could go to the PepsiWorld site to see which artists were new to the program. They could even sample the music that they could order through this program. You could do a 30-second download, play the music and decide what you wanted. This drove our traffic up tremendously.

If we tried this on packaging that has to be produced six months ahead, this would have been impossible.

In addition to Yahoo!, we are also involved in another partnership, a company called Bolt.com, which is a huge teen site. It's another content site we've selected that really attracts the right consumers for us and it's not only just through banner ads, but by sponsoring polls and being an integral part of the site itself.

At this time, few companies have the vision or the resources to really handle branding online in a compelling way. Brands such as Yahoo! and Amazon know how to use online marketing to their advantage, but most traditional consumer packaged goods companies are not as well equipped for this. Only a few companies, such as Kellogg's, Unilever, Kraft and Procter & Gamble are doing it quite well.

We believe that the Internet plays to our strengths in terms of creating entertainment and excitement. The visual look clearly is getting better and better and you can do more and more things on the web. We think this benefits us because our brands are very visual and our imagery is very visual. We are trying to use the medium more aggressively than our competitors. We think it's a great opportunity to build loyalty for our brands if we do it the right way. I believe we're off to a great start.

Our packaging is part of this, but I doubt the Internet will change our package design. We can change our design, our logos and our look online because the Internet so dynamic. We can do things that are fun, exciting and different. It could allow consumers to customize the look of their products if you want to go that far. The customer could actually go online to PepsiWorld and design his or her own Pepsi label. For example, you could put a picture of your family on the label, print the label out and wrap it around your bottles. Or, if my daughter Katie had a birthday party, the label could say "Happy Birthday, Katie" and it could even have a picture of Katie on the Pepsi bottle. We think it could be a fun thing.

But, will it change our primary packages? No. What the interactive world allows us to do online is to have some fun because people expect us to do that. But for our package in the offline world, the grocery store and the convenience store, we do not see any major differences in package design anytime soon.

There are different ways of selling consumer products on the Internet. One is to sell directly to the consumer. In our business, we really can't for two reasons. First, our franchisees are all entrepreneurs who have exclusive rights to certain geographies. If, for example, somebody in St. Louis goes online and wants to buy a case of Pepsi products from us directly, we cannot do that. We cannot ship products that we make in New York to a customer in St. Louis because the regional bottler has the rights to that customer. Second, it is very expensive to ship our type of products to customers directly. The profit margins are relatively small so that this just would not work.

However, there are companies that are shipping groceries to your house. But one of the things that makes us so strong at Pepsi and Frito-Lay is that we have such great relationships with a lot of grocers. We can go into grocery stores and merchandise very well. When you walk into a grocery store you will see Pepsi displays on the front end and you will see the Frito-Lay display on the perimeter. This is going to drive a lot of impulse purchases around the store because people see our products.

When you order online, it's very different. A lot of times the products are listed alphabetically. So we can't use our merchandising muscle and our ability to really dress up stores and create in-store theater that benefits the retailers and benefits us.

But I do think that Internet grocers are onto something. While going to the stores can be entertaining, the biggest issue facing people today is the time press. People just don't have the time to go shopping the way they used to. It's a hassle. If you can have your purchases delivered to your house it can be much easier. There is a social experience that some people will find really important and valuable. But it's not going to change overnight. People tend to change very slowly. A lot of people will resist shopping for groceries online and many online retailers cannot provide the kind of service they should and still make money.

Consumers still want to feel and touch perishables. And, when people go somewhere and buy perishables, they might as well just load up on everything else too. When they walk into a grocery store with a list, I guarantee you that they will walk out with more than was on their list.

When you order from an Internet grocer, your list is made from a standard list and you push a button. You're not doing a lot of impulse shopping online. Grocers can't create the impulse sales on the Internet that grocers normally do in the store. I think that what they will ultimately have to do is start with groceries, but then offer everything from DVDs to CDs to stuff from the Gap. They will have to build the infrastructure for a distribution system that could economically deliver items to the home. If they can make that happen, they will no longer be competing with Grand Union or A&P or Safeway.

Our challenge will be to figure out how to work with retailers to help them on their site, so that we can create excitement and impulse sales. We can help our retailers by finding ways to create interest and excitement through online contests and different things to get people engaged so that they buy more impulse items online.

Overseas, the shopping experience is different. For instance, British-based retailers are much more consolidated and have a much better shopping experience with consumers. The retailers in Europe have a lot of clout. Two or three big retailers control all Europe, and therefore I am not sure whether online grocery shopping would work as well there – the infrastructure is not in place.

There are many avenues for promoting your products effectively on the Internet. But first we need to break out of this mindset that broadcast advertising – specifically TV advertising – is the only way to do this. There still exists a mentality that TV is critical and you want to protect your TV spending as much as possible. We need to recognize that we must be more aggressive. Right now, we spend about 2–5% of our total advertising budget online. That number has to grow to 10 or 20%. We need to break the mentality that the Internet is not as effective or as powerful as other media and find a way to invest more in that area.

Second, we must explore how much we can invest on the Internet and how we can do it in a way that's really suitable to that medium. Right now, we do it in a way where we're just taking our traditional thinking and applying it to the Internet. But it will take new thinking and new ways to build brands.

Advertising people are so afraid that they don't get much from banner advertising – that it does not drive the businesses, have the reach, or the production values you get from TV. I think that is partly because the old guard still controls the traditional ad agencies. On the one hand, they are getting into more interactive business, but on the other hand, they try to discourage spending too much money online. They feel it hurts their revenue stream and runs contrary to what traditional advertising is all about, which is creating big budget, high production value and exciting TV commercials.

However, while the networks are still getting more money every year, they are losing more and more business to all the other outlets. Network TV was 79–80% of the advertising business ten years ago. Now it's more like 45%.

But, there's still a mindset that leans toward mass marketing and mass advertising. Everybody understands TV. Few understand how to create online excitement and swing investment that way. It takes working with the right agencies and the right people to help to create the right ideas that fit that medium. I think that is going to be the biggest challenge we face today and in the immediate future. This is as true for PepsiCo as, I think, it is true for a lot of consumer package goods companies.

Some of the old mindsets will be challenged by how much competitors will be changing. Companies will react to what their major competitors are doing. Competition often forces you to do it. You start to look at the numbers. There are so many hours in the day, so many hours that people digest media. We see the numbers shifting toward the Internet.

And, there is another important development in interfacing with the consumer: electronic devices, such as cell phones and Palm Pilots. These could make online shopping even better because people could do it even away from home.

We research people's buying habits and what they are doing on the run. While there are many people who are not online yet, I believe that they will be shortly. We want to know their shopping habits. When people register for PepsiStuff.com, we send them a questionnaire with about seven or eight questions such as whether they are male or female; what age they are; how many soft drinks they purchase in a week; what their favorite brand is; what their last ten purchases were; how many of these were Pepsi; how many Coke; how many Mountain Dew; how many Sprite; and also what they are interested in – music, sports, and so forth. They get 500 points for answering these basic questions, and we have a real database of people with whom we can then communicate.

We could do all sorts of different things for our consumers. Consumers can email us and tell us what they like and don't like, and if they wish we would have more of certain products. If we are launching a new Pepsi line extension, we could ask the consumer whether it should be Lemon Pepsi, or Lime Pepsi, or Raspberry Pepsi. What should it be? What would you prefer? We can actually develop the final flavor based on what the consumer wants. We can create whole new product ideas based on what the consumers are asking for.

Pepsi can also use this database to email everybody saying "Great news! Lemon Pepsi or Pepsi Twist is coming this summer." This is fully interactive communication. This is really going to be very strong in the future. The beauty of promoting through the Internet is that we can actually change the promotion as we go. We have the capability to react quickly to the consumer. If we did this through a direct mail program, it would be very expensive. It's one thing if you are promoting Porsches through direct mail, but with low margin products it doesn't pay out.

So, in that way the consumer has more control over how we market our products. It's much more customized. The consumer is absolutely the big winner here in terms of the value and actually getting what they want from us.

It's an opportunity for people to really engage in our promotions and to know more and more quickly about our promotions. It is a way of quickly gauging a Pepsi promotion versus a Sprite commercial. And this forces us to offer as much value as possible to your consumer. For example, Pizza Hut ran a program where when you bought a pizza you got $30 off at AOL shopping. So for a $10 purchase, you got a $30 benefit. We better make sure that our value is at least equal to their value. That's the challenge in comparison shopping. We want to make sure that we are competitive with our programs.

The Internet, unquestionably, will play the role of shaping and building brands. The Internet will become a very important way to enrich people's lives and become part of people's lifestyle. Brands that want to be a part of these lifestyles need to be online in order to connect with the consumer. Companies will recognize this more and more and will find ways to utilize the nature of the Internet to connect with consumers. Otherwise, they will be seen as yesterday's brands. In the next few years, it will be critical for brands to take advantage of the power that the Internet provides to communicate to consumers what their brands are all about.

jonathannelson

Jonathan Nelson

Co-founder and Chief Executive Officer

organicinc.

As Chief Executive Officer of Organic, Jonathan Nelson has led the company to help major corporations, online start-ups and non-profit organizations tap the enormous potential of the Internet. Jonathan co-founded Organic in 1993, before the first web browser was born, and he has founded or played a critical role in building a number of other companies, ranging from an early 1990s cyber cafe and performance space to one of the first online yellow pages services. Jonathan has helped to establish the Internet as a revolutionary economic catalyst and has been recognized for his visionary ideas and innovative thinking by international publications. He was named one of the top 100 young innovators of the century by MIT's *Technology Review* in 1999.

10 interfacing with advertising

Many people really look at e-branding as distinct and different from traditional branding. And there are certain elements that may be different, but once it starts to become mainstream, then traditional branding will encompass what is now e-branding and people will just call it "business."

To gain consumer confidence online, you need to create a very tight filter around the customer value proposition. Ultimately, the Internet has shifted the balance of power from retailers, producers of goods and services over to the purchaser. What the Internet has really done is erased a lot of geography and given the choice to the people. We're all competing with a subset of competitors that we've never seen before, because the Internet is strictly global and will get more global over time. In this highly fragmented, competitive market where geography is erased, we really have to hit customers with our best shot up front, and say what it is that the customers want. What value do they want from me? Do they simply want the best price, the most relevant information, a combination of best price and relevant information in a context of a totally useable interface which is updated regularly for me? These are the types of questions that I think brands really need to think about constantly.

> *"Advertising not measured by Nielson has heretical ramifications, and accountability will be the big day of reckoning online. We can tie the marketing directly to the purchases, and understand how customers are managed in the online environment."*

I'm not advocating that every company has to have an entirely personalized site in its native language. For example, a company making door stoppers may be out of context. They could talk about the advanced polymer plastics used to make the door stoppers or the advanced door stopper shape, but at the end of the day they're still making door stoppers. Should they really have a high profile, high cost website? They may be better off selling the product through an office supply company, that'll have five types of door stoppers from which to pick. I assume it will often be based on price. So, that might be the future for some types of brands or companies. You've seen companies struggle hard to try to build a brand around what is just a commodity, and yet conversely you've seen other companies actively differentiate themselves because they truly have points of difference and can use the Internet effectively to show these points. Particularly companies with "perishable" information. Yahoo! is a great example of a content intermediary in some cases, a content provider in others, a true portal or a search engine. They make theirs a one-stop shop. Or, take the analogy of E∗TRADE. The stock market is changing literally moment by moment. E∗TRADE is your window into that world, and they have your personal permission, portfolio and so forth. So, in some ways the brand itself becomes just part of your life. You don't obsess about E∗TRADE or Yahoo!, you just go there to your screen. It's synonymous with everything you do.

At Organic, we have an interesting experience going on right now with an automobile company which involves discussions about what automobile companies do on the web besides giving the latest information on models and pricing and so forth. Think of how you can connect the dealers, you can do procurements, you have B to B applications, extranets and consumer-facing applications. And beyond that, what should they become in the future? How about telematics bringing wireless into automobiles? Do you really want to trade stocks from your car? From a brand perspective, should my automobile company be thought of as a personal transportation business? Will I really look to them to provide stock trading utilities and be my portal? So, how does the brand extend itself, and what is the customer value proposition?

Auto parts can be great for the web. If you really are in the personal trans-portation business, you should maintain my personal vehicle and, in many cases, the relationship. Since brands are about relationships, why not monitor and maintain my vehicle for me? The automobile could self-diagnose, which a lot of automobiles do, but you can go one step further using wireless technology to book an appointment with the dealership or repair company, and then get a list of options. In the future, you can see on your wireless email the scheduling of five appointments that have been done for you. And you can pick one by pressing a button. That would be wonderful and it's what a company in the future should do. It's maintaining a section of my life, in this case, the personal transportation section. Do that for me!

In discussing the subject of branding, I'll probably put my foot in my mouth with regard to a lot of the classic branding. But, whether in the digital space, or in the traditional space, a brand is still a promise. And, whether it's a mark of quality, integrity, or value, it's still a promise of some sort, because you'll take this empty vessel, which is a mark and a word, and endow it with some attributes that are abstract reminders of what will come. This makes it a promise. In the online space, the thing that strikes me is that the brand and the promise become synonymous with each other, because when you have branding online, you're one click away from the promise. The way you interact with something, and the way that you use it, become part of the value proposition, and it's woven together in a way that's different from the analog space.

You also might say that there are two kinds of brands. There are these upstart brands such as Yahoo! and AOL, and then there are the existing brands such as Coke or Pepsi who are trying to figure out what they should do. It's a big challenge for packaged goods companies to really have a brand proposition which is beyond their tagline, once they get into the online environment, versus a bank or a place where you can do online trading. Take the upstart "E∗TRADE" versus the "DLJ Direct." It's an interesting counter-point of two brands with which you can be interactive and the brand is personified right there in the online environment. Then take Pepsi, which you're not going to drink online. Maybe you'll get Pepsi points or something like that, but the actual brand gratification experience will be quite different.

There are ways, however, that you can get a gratification experience with packaged goods. For example, I think of orange juice for a couple of reasons. One, is that I'm thirsty. I won't get gratified for my thirst in the online environment. Another reason for thinking of orange juice is wanting to be healthy – I won't get Vitamin C from the online environment unless it comes through the radiation on my screen. But there is orange juice information that is gratifying which can come from the online environment, because maybe there is something special about the way it's freshly squeezed. Perhaps it comes from special groves of oranges. There may be some sort of promotional component to the orange juice that ties the online and the offline together. I personally think that generally it'll be a bit less gratifying than the interactivity of Yahoo! or E*TRADE, but that doesn't mean it won't be gratifying at all. So the future will have levels of gratification. Some brands may be completely synonymous with gratification and live online only, such as Yahoo!. Some brands which are very analog and successful as offline brands can export a little bit to become more online.

With any of these brands, especially for packaged goods, the value proposition can bring it to the top. Certain brands have made a brilliant franchise out of what is arguably a simple commodity. Evian Water, for instance, created a brilliant brand which they can reinforce through the mountain glaciers, lakes, wells and whatever, and can wrap themselves around this, online. Coke and Levi's can wrap themselves around youth events, and Nike around sporting events, online. And this promotional nature will enable these brands to take advantage of the web.

We've seen a lot of companies embarrass themselves. They go out there and make up value propositions, or try to overblow themselves – like the detergent company that had a stain detector feature on its website. I thought that website was absurd. When I spill blueberry jam all over the front of my shirt, I don't need to go to the web to figure out what it is.

Before Organic, I had very little experience in advertising, and today, I have incredible respect for those directors who can make you cry in 30 seconds or less. There are brilliant brands out there and it's unbelievable how certain brands have their allegiances, whether it's Gucci, Prada, Nike or the 150-year-old Levi's. The brand adds such a huge component to it. Branding, particularly through traditional advertising, is a lot about creating auras for customer acquisition and making people feel good about the purchases that they've made. Advertising has really been built around the media that carry it. So undoubtedly, you do different things between print and television and outdoor and radio. There are different ways in which to advertise. For example, outdoor is all about size and space and, interestingly, it is about the time it takes to drive past something, versus TV in which you have a choice of 15-second, 30-second or one-minute segments. These all tend to be broadcast-type media.

Online, you're there interacting with the brand. The interesting thing about interactive is that it is exactly what it sounds like. It is interactive and that shifts advertising and branding a lot. Online, you're starting to see it shift and move from motivation to customer acquisition. With online marketing, there is purchasing through banners or buttons or whatever. You can maintain a relationship. When Yahoo! sells you a banner, they sell you real estate on which you can put whatever you want. You can do targeted advertising, you can do broadcast advertising. You can make a request, get the information in the space of the banner and continue on Yahoo!. That's the kind of thing you'll see move in the future. And online will become very focused and specific, because interactive is addressable. And with TV and radio moving into digital, they'll look more like interactive and they too will be addressable. We're truly going to get the right message to the right person at the right time in the right kind of situation. And I think that will kick the whole world wide open. All of a sudden a trillion dollars a year which is spent in traditional advertising – a majority of which is spent in radio and television – is focused in a more online, live-based, absolutely certifiable metrics environment. You will know whether your customers are just browsing constantly or whether they are purchasers. And if they're purchasers, what level are they? Are they our really highly valued customer or do they just come once and never return?

Right now, if I advertise on the Super Bowl, I'm spending several million dollars to know that I'm hitting 50 million households. Online, you absolutely know where you stand, the accountability of online gets poured into television, and you look at your media buying completely differently. Your messaging will be more segmented and accountable.

Media online today is liquid. It's kind of a wild west right now. There are few standards. There are banners, buttons, sponsored content, email, and many more options. And you can click on just about any of this and connect to other content and other e-banners. We're putting banners on some client sites to hyper-link them to other parts of the site. And right now banners are probably the most commonly accepted form of frontline Internet advertising. But at Organic, we're trying to really push the boundaries of the medium. And a lot of this is through real estate, since big pieces of real estate tend to get people's attention, as in outdoor advertising. If it's in your face and it's well targeted − even if it's not well targeted − you'll pay attention. But beyond that, I think you play into the value proposition. For instance, if I knew you were looking at a site and I had a relationship with you, I would target you with different information from somebody who is going to the site for the first time. For instance, if I'm representing a financial services company, and you already have an account with them, I'll either try not to target you at all, so that I can spend my ad dollars on customer acquisition, or I'll try to maintain my relationship with you by giving you pertinent information based on your needs. This type of targeting is really the next step and where we're going with the Internet.

In my opinion, we're going to see interactive and television slowly come together. You'll be able to stop your TV and go to the ad, which in some cases will be synonymous with the program. Convergence is probably the best word ever, because that's really what is happening here. And that gets really interesting. You'll carry around a network cell phone, you'll be networked at your desktop at work, so you'll always be online. Now you're one person. The challenge for these brands is addressing you in each of your environments. How do I not waste your time? After all, the brand is still a promise of quality. Time is one of the most critical and valuable quantities that any of us have, so how do we touch in each of these spots with relevant information that is valuable to you and that adds to our relationship? That's a big part of the value proposition.

There's a very interesting component when you think about advertising not being measured by Nielson. That has heretical ramifications, and accountability will be the big day of reckoning online. We can tie the marketing directly to the purchases, and understand how customers are managed in the online environment. This completely shifts the strategies. One, you come out with more messages to see what works in terms of measurable contribution to a business's bottom line, as though you're in a giant focus group. You are constantly innovating, changing, evolving and trying to balance supply and demand in terms of pricing and other things. The entire advertising strategy will shift and the way the money is spent will shift. The messages will shift and become more segmented. This idea of empowering customers with the Internet has the genie out of the bottle and it is just going to keep moving.

In the early days of the Internet, the myth was that any company can start with a "level playing field." Well, the bottom line is that GE still has hundreds of millions of dollars to spend on marketing, and most people in their bedrooms don't. I was working with a senior VP marketing for a huge fast-food company early in the Internet business, and we were working late one night when he threw up his hands in exasperation and said, "I see where this is going. Life used to be so easy. When we bought three networks and ten magazines, we hit 85% of the country. And now we have sixty channels of television, infinite magazines, and the Internet's coming and there literally will be millions of other channels." Well, that's exactly what's going to happen. The Super Bowl will always aggregate huge audiences and networks will always have big audiences, but you'll also see a niche for everything, and a great majority of those will be advertising opportunities. And brands will have to respond to the very nature of the way that this whole right message, right time and right person meet the different places where people spend their time. You need to start to juggle all of these things, and hit them with relevant pieces of information each step of the way. If you really want to hit that niche audience with the perfect message, you may find the perfect website for it. And your advertising, while still a relatively large part of your budget, will need to be incredibly focused.

Brands can start to have relationships with customers where there is no intermediary. You do not need Yahoo! once you've got a customer's email address or once they've allowed you into their life. In a sense, the intermediaries supply the customer, serve up the customer in the beginning, but it's up to you to keep the dialogue going once you've got them, which has pretty interesting ramifications. Think about advertising where there's no media buy involved. Or is it advertising? You've given me your email and I'm doing relationship management, giving you value propositions by telling you about specials. There's no Yahoo! or *New York Times* involved here. We have a relationship now. And brands need to get the customer's attention, keep the relationship and stay relevant. Right now brands are promises. Maybe an interesting idea about e-branding is that brands become stronger relationships. Not that the promise goes away, but the relationship becomes much more interactive.

Another form of online relationships are the partnerships that emerge through the Internet. The partners are looking for brand recognition and you need to give as much as you get. You can either go an inch deep and a mile wide or a mile deep and an inch wide and you see different strategies being played out. At one time, CBS MarketWatch was a private company that gave up a huge amount of equity to get that CBS brand name and to be on the morning show with Bryant Gumbel. Everything that CBS does for advertising is a mile deep and an inch wide versus Yahoo!, who is doing partnerships with people all over the place. I think you want to affiliate yourself with like-minded companies and be associated so that your brands are recognized. It seems to be good strategy thus far, but we'll see as this thing plays out more.

With online partnerships, as well as online information and transactions, reliability and accurate information will always be important. I think you will see safe places to go like the Disney portal for children. AOL runs everything through a filter. There will be a certain amount of regulation, but some things will get through, since it's easy to put up a website. But you have to look at the cost benefit overall, and for great content the value proposition far outweighs the disadvantages. The wild west was untamed for a long time. Then slowly, when people figured it out and put structure around it, it came into check.

Advertising has been an interesting experience for me and I have a huge respect for advertising, since it's an incredibly involved art form. We're trying to take the "e" out of e-business and bridge the interactive island into the mainstream world. And this necessitates our clients looking across many media to wherever our customer is. Advertising is in for a pretty big sea-change, in my opinion. And the concept of sales promotion is also starting to change. You can't turn on the TV and look at a sporting event without seeing a sign on the field for www.whatever.com. You're seeing that cross-promotion and when you go to those sites, hopefully, they have something that ties in to the sport event and is relevant.

The accountability will force a lot of people into a day of reckoning. In a sense, direct marketing, which had been the second stepchild of advertising, has really smart ideas with a lot of lessons to be learned. In some ways, I think direct marketing is closer to what we will be doing than, let's say, television advertising. Accountability, and the metrics and those ideas are all going to be really relevant. Brands will need to hone down on their core value propositions. And we will look at how each of the available media is used effectively to touch the customer with relevant, valuable information, utility, education, or commerce. Accountability is your life blood and the Internet gives advertising the opportunity to really focus.

allanpoulter
moiradmacdonald

Allan Poulter
Managing Director

markforceassociates

Morag Macdonald
Partner

bird&bird

Allan Poulter is a Registered Trade Mark Attorney and the Managing Director of Markforce Associates in London, having joined the company from Marks & Clerk where he was a partner from 1995. He is co-author of *A User's Guide to Trade Marks and Passing-Off* published by Butterworth's, the co-editor of *The Community Trade Mark* published by INTA, and a frequent lecturer both in the UK and overseas on trade mark law, practice and related issues.

Morag Macdonald joined the Intellectual Property Department of Bird & Bird in 1985, having trained as a barrister, and became a partner of the firm in 1989. Her particular interests are a peculiar and unusual mixture of trade marks with computers and electronics and associated law. Her degree, from Cambridge University, was in Mathematics, Physics and Law and she has programmed in a range of 3GL languages including Fortran, Basic and Assembler. She has dealt with a number of complaints under the ICANN UDRP including the well-known case concerning jeanettewinterson.com.

11

brand identity **and the law**

Introduction

On one level the legal issues relevant to e-commerce and branding are the same as with traditional trade since it is not the underlying business activity that has changed but rather the medium through which trade is conducted. However, there is something of a dichotomy between the potentially international nature of e-commerce and the national territorial scope of registered trade mark protection.

The speed with which e-commerce has developed and been embraced has not been matched by corresponding amendments to legislation. The law is notorious for being slow to adapt to changing commercial conditions and this is no more clearly demonstrated than in relation to the protection and enforcement of trade mark rights. Indeed, as legislation is gradually introduced to address these issues throughout the world, new previously unrecognized problems arise requiring further amendment or adaptation. Furthermore, the nature of the e-commerce beast, particularly when dealing with new start-up companies, is such that everything has do be done yesterday, which can also create problems. All this means that lawyers advising on trade mark law and other legal issues relating to e-commerce and the protection of brands will have to be efficient, adaptable and possibly even creative!

> *"From a branding perspective, the advent of e-commerce has understandably brought the ownership of domain names to the forefront of many companies' marketing initiatives."*

There are two separate yet related key legal issues that need to be addressed when considering the future of e-branding. The first is the question of obtaining protection of one's brand name in the countries where trade is, or is likely to be, conducted and the consideration of what other distinctive features of a business, in addition to the brand name, can be protected. The second issue is the enforcement of those rights secured against unauthorized use of conflicting marks by third parties.

Protection

The Internet has enabled traders of all sizes to have the potential of targeting consumers far beyond the traditional national geographic boundaries that once would have represented a natural limit to their trading activities. The main tool utilized by a trader to protect his brand has been the securing of registered trade mark rights within the trader's home country, which generally would have been sufficient. Any move into export markets would normally have been gradual and planned well in advance, enabling searches of local registers to be conducted and the filing of appropriate applications for registration to be made. This also meant that the associated cost of searching and filing was necessarily spread over a reasonably long period. Now, the potential for immediate international exposure of one's brand has dramatically reduced this development period.

The advent of e-commerce has created many new would-be entrepreneurs and has given existing local traders international aspirations. From a branding perspective this has understandably brought the ownership of domain names to the forefront of many companies' marketing initiatives.

It is a commonly held yet mistaken belief that the ownership of the domain name (particularly the dot.com) provides the proprietor with all the protection that is needed to enable trade to commence unhindered throughout the world and provide an enforceable monopoly right in the name within the proprietor's area of commercial activity. If only it were so simple. The reality is that the ownership of the top level domain (TLD), although undoubtedly an attractive and valuable commercial asset, does not provide the proprietor with any rights in the name other than the ability to prevent another party from obtaining the identical name as a domain name. The limited value of the ownership of a domain name, from a legal perspective, will become even more apparent with the proliferation of TLD designations.

To secure protection of a brand name it generally remains necessary to obtain national trade mark registrations in each of the countries of interest. Needless to say, the cost of such a filing programme can be prohibitively expensive, particularly for a start-up venture with limited capital. However, there have been some developments towards simplifying the securing of international or multinational protection. Within the European Union it is now possible to secure a single registration affording protection within each of the countries of the EU. A "Community trade mark" application is filed at the Office for Harmonization of the Internal Market (OHIM) based in Alicante, Spain. This has greatly simplified the procedure for protecting a mark within the EU and significantly reduced the cost of securing and maintaining a European trade mark portfolio. It is ideally suited to e-traders.

For many years there has also been in existence an "international" registration procedure (the Madrid Agreement and subsequent Protocol). Unlike the Community trade mark, an international registration is not a single registration as such but rather a system for filing national applications in signatory countries through a single application filed at the World Intellectual Property Organization (WIPO). The system provides a cheaper, and in some countries quicker, method of securing national registrations in the designated countries. The effectiveness of the international registration procedure has been limited to date, due to the fact that many of the important trading nations are not signatories to the Madrid Agreement or Protocol. However, with the recent joining by Japan and Singapore and the anticipated accession by the US (with the likelihood of other countries following suit), the system will quickly become the favoured route for companies seeking international protection of their brands. Again, this is a particularly welcome development for e-traders and will significantly reduce the cost of obtaining necessary international protection of brands.

Unfortunately, the international and Community trade mark registration systems do not negate the need to conduct trade mark clearance searches of the national registers of each country prior to the use of a mark. It remains imperative that, prior to any move into new territories, searches of the local registers are conducted in order to assess any infringement risk associated with the proposed launch. Part of the problem with e-commerce and start-up companies in particular is the speed with which a project moves from simply being an idea to its implementation. The process of selecting a new brand name is generally undertaken within very short time scales which often means that the clearance process cannot be staged. This results in significantly increased and otherwise avoidable costs. This is compounded by the need to search in a large number of jurisdictions. Indeed, the usual answer given to the question "in which countries will you be trading?" is "global". In order to develop a commercially viable and practicable search and filing strategy, it is essential that a realistic assessment of the likely geographical scope of the business be made.

It seems unlikely that in the foreseeable future there will be any way of short-circuiting the search and filing process. Although the extension of the Madrid Agreement to more territories is likely to continue, there is little likelihood of any imminent move towards a global trade mark right.

Registrable trade marks

Traditionally, the distinctive characteristics of a business that have been protected through trade mark registration were limited to the brand name itself and/or a logo. However, in recent years, legislation in many jurisdictions has been implemented to recognize that other features of a business can distinguish the goods and services of one undertaking from those of another. The test widely adopted is that any such sign that is capable of distinguishing, and which can be represented graphically (a requirement which recognizes the need to have a register which can easily be searched in order to identify clearly the extent of the monopoly right granted), can be the subject of a trade mark registration. Although there are exceptions to this general rule, the result is that we now have the situation where many national registries are accepting registrations of sound marks, smells, slogans, the get-up of retail premises and packaging, colours and gestures.

There is no reason, in principle, why this list will not be extended to include other distinctive elements used in the course of e-trade such as animated trade marks, amorphous marks, holograms and the distinctive get-up of a website. Registrars may, initially, be reluctant to grant registrations for such marks although if the mark satisfies the basic requirement of a trade mark, in that it serves to denote the origin of the goods/services of the proprietor, there is no reason why registration should not be secured.

One difficulty that will be faced in securing registration of such marks will be the requirement for the applicant adequately to describe his mark graphically, so that the ambit of the protection sought can be clearly identified and the existence of the mark located by a reasonable search strategy. Clearly, randomly changing marks would necessarily be incapable of such description.

It is likely that, in the future, traditional trade marks (particularly word marks) will continue to dominate. However, traders should consider carefully other elements of their business model or the manner in which they trade to ensure that any such features that serve to distinguish their business from competitors are suitably protected.

In addition to registered trade mark protection, there is also the possibility that the distinctive signs used by a business (other than word marks) may be the subject of copyright protection. Generally speaking, copyright subsists in an original work from the moment of its creation and (subject to certain exceptions) vests in the creator of the work. Therefore, if the work in question has been created by an independent contractor, rather than an employee of the company, it would be advisable to secure an assignment of the copyright at the earliest opportunity to enable appropriate action to be taken to prevent any unauthorized copying of the work without the need to involve the original owner. However, the existence of copyright protection should not be used as an excuse to refrain from securing trade mark registrations as it is not possible to rely on copyright to prevent the use of a confusingly similar mark where that mark has been created quite independently and where there has been no actual copying.

With a little thought, and by taking appropriate legal advice at an early stage in the development of a business model or the launch of a new product or service, it should be possible to ensure that the best protection of a brand name and other distinctive features of a business is secured within sensible time scales and a reasonable budget.

Enforcement – where to go

When a trade mark owner has a problem with the registration of a domain name by someone else they need to know where to go to get the matter dealt with. This issue breaks down into two essential categories. The first of these concerns the generic top level domains such as dot.com, dot.net and dot.org. The second concerns the numerous geographical TLDs such as dot.fr, dot.tv, dot.com, dot.au and dot.co.uk. This is because the geographical TLDs are administered by independent registrars based in the country to which the designation relates. Each of these registrars has its own rules and regulations about how it deals with domain name disputes. Meanwhile, as far as the generic TLDs are concerned, the registrars administering these all comply with the ICANN (Internet Corporation for Assigned Names and Numbers) UDRPs (Uniform Domain Name Dispute Resolution Policy).

Domain name disputes can be dealt with either by way of a dispute resolution procedure adopted by the relevant domain name registrar administering the domain name in question (if such exists) and/or through the courts of the relevant country or countries. The ICANN UDRP which is discussed below has, despite only having been operative since the beginning of 2000, proved to be quite an effective procedure for trade mark owners. However, in general, the dispute resolution procedures adopted by many of the geographical TLD registrars are still not proving to be as effective. In some cases, some of the geographical TLDs have also signed up to the ICANN UDRP and there is discussion of further geographical TLD registrars signing up to this. However, currently this is still an issue for trade mark owners.

Many courts throughout the world in their decisions recognize the issues concerning domain name hijacking or cyber squatting. Where necessary, laws have been adapted to make it possible for courts to at least order the transfer of domain names where they believe that they have been registered by a third party who should not be entitled to hold that domain name. The US has gone so far as to introduce legislation to deal with cyber squatting, although to date such additional specific legislation has not been introduced by other countries. When a trade mark owner is considering court action against someone who they believe is cyber squatting, the normal rule is to go to the court which has jurisdiction over that third party. That court will be the court where the third party is resident. In some incidences that is not a particularly satisfactory country for the trade mark owners to bring proceedings into court and, therefore, there can be other choices available to them such as the court of the country in which the relevant domain name registrar is based or, in certain circumstances, the country where the server holding the website to which the domain name is delegated is situated or the country where the domain name is infringing the trade mark. The only difficulty with the last two options is that while the trade mark owner may obtain a court order, this may prove to be ineffective for a number of reasons. If nothing else, courts in other countries will not enforce such an order unless the relevant treaty is in place between the countries of the courts in question to require this.

The ICANN UDRP

At the beginning of the year 2000, the UDRP was put into place for domain name disputes relating to the generic top level domains such as dot.com, dot.net and dot.org. Certain organizations were approved by ICANN to administer this procedure. Among these was the WIPO and, in particular, its arbitration centre.

UDRP lays down rules concerning the means by which a dispute can be brought before one of the designated dispute resolution centres and concerning the basis on which a decision can be given, either requiring the domain name registrant to transfer the domain name to the complainant or not as the case may be. The procedure is relatively cheap and quick. The various dispute resolution centres charge the complainant in the order of a few thousand dollars (depending on the number of arbitrators designated; one or three). From the time of filing the dispute, a timetable is set so that a decision is rendered within a maximum of nine weeks except in exceptional circumstances.

The rules require that a complainant show that the domain name registrant registered the domain name in dispute on a non-bona fide basis and is continuing to hold it on a non-bona fide basis and that that person is not entitled to the domain name. The main basis for any such complaint is normally a trade mark registration but this does not necessarily have to be the case. There have been some decisions based on unregistered trade marks where the trade mark owner was able to show that they had such trade mark rights and that such rights were more than local. By contrast, the mere ownership of a registered trade mark will not guarantee success for a complainant. There have been a number of decisions now in favour of the respondent where the respondent was able to demonstrate some form of bona fide interest in the domain name and, in particular, where the trade mark owner could not show any reputation of his trade mark beyond one country. Normally the arbitrators who have presided over these disputes have felt it necessary to take into consideration the international nature of the Internet and, therefore, do take into consideration the existence of a lack of any reputation in a number of countries.

An example of the ICANN UDRP in operation was the case concerning the domain name jeanettewinterson.com. Jeanette Winterson is an English writer who is published in over 21 countries in the world in a variety of languages. An academic with Cambridge University registered her name as a dot.com along with some 130 other English authors' names. Needless to say, Ms Winterson did not have her name registered as a trade mark but was not about to have it hijacked just as she was about to launch her new hi-tech inspired book *The Powerbook*. Fortunately, Jeanette Winterson is hardly a common name and she launched a UDRP complaint based on her considerable reputation. Within just a few weeks the WIPO appointed arbitrator found in her favour and required the domain name to be transferred to her. The cost of the procedure was a few thousand dollars and the result was achieved, on a worldwide basis of course, in a fraction of the time that it would have taken for a series of national courts to deal with the matter.

Misuse of trade marks on the Internet

Domain name cyber squatting is not the only type of misuse of trade marks which can be seen on the Internet. Straight trade mark infringement is now rife. It is not at all uncommon for a trade mark owner to find blatant infringement of his trade marks by others on their websites.

However, there are also less obvious forms of trade mark infringement which can occur on the Internet. A good example of this is the use of trade marks in "meta-tags". What this involves is the relevant trade mark not appearing on the part of the website which can be seen by a viewer but being put into the software code of that website so that the software from indexing pages, search engines and web callers see the trade mark. The effect of this is that, for example, when using a search engine to find a website relating to a particular trade mark, those websites with a trade mark appearing in their meta-tags will appear high up the list in search results. Indeed, clever meta-tagging by trade mark infringers can mean that their website appears higher in the search results than that of the legitimate trade mark owners. As far as courts are concerned, this is a relatively new phenomenon for them to tackle and only a few around the world have issued decisions relating to trade mark infringement through meta-tags. However, of those who have applied themselves to the issue, the uniform view appears to be that this does indeed amount to trade mark infringement even though the potential consumer never actually sees the trade mark itself.

Another version of this phenomenon is referred to as "word stuffing". This involves inserting the trade mark being misused into the HTML code behind the website on a frequent basis, so that once again the indexing software, and some search engine software, recognizes the website in question in preference to that with fewer mentions of the trade mark. Based on the court decisions which do exist concerning trade mark infringement by meta-tagging, it seems likely that courts will also find this particular misuse of trade marks to be an infringement.

Disclaimers

The other side of the coin to misuse of trade marks on the Internet is a concern on the part of companies that they might unintentionally infringe the trade marks of another. This becomes a particular issue where, due to the territorial nature of trade mark registrations, one organization owns the same trade mark as another but in relation to a different country or set of countries. Since the Internet knows no national boundaries, this has arisen as a particular issue for companies using the Internet.

One of the interesting things about trade marks, however, is that in general a registered trade mark will only be infringed if the person using it is actually using it for trading purposes in the country where it is registered. Thus, if a trade mark is registered in the UK and that same trade mark is being used on a Finnish language website in relation to the same goods or services for which the UK trade mark is registered but directed specifically at the Finnish marketplace, there is a good argument to say that this does not amount to infringement of the UK registered trade mark. This is because the trade mark is not being used in the course of trade in the UK. This argument can be reinforced by way of a disclaimer. Thus, it is possible to make it clear on the relevant website that the goods and services being sold under a particular trade mark are not available for sale in another country where that trade mark is registered. Such disclaimers can be particularly useful where one cannot point to the language of the website as distinguishing the market-place to which that website is directed. This, clearly, can be a particular issue for English language and increasingly Spanish language websites in particular. However, such disclaimers will not save a website owner where, in fact, they are not acting in accordance with a disclaimer. If a website says that the goods on offer are not available for sale in the US, but nevertheless accepts and fulfills orders for consumers clearly resident in the US, all the disclaimers in the world will not save you from the inevitable conclusion that the site is actually trading in the US.

It has to be said that disclaimers of this type have not been extensively tested yet in the courts of various countries in the world and, therefore, it still remains to be seen the extent to which they can assist. However, if such disclaimers are not found by courts to be effective, it is difficult to see how the Internet community will deal with the issue of cross-border trade mark infringement where the old world of trade mark laws is rubbing up against the new world of e-commerce.

Conclusion

Clearly, branding in a virtual world is here to stay. As technologies expand and develop, branding becomes more important as a signpost for business and the related legal issues will expand and develop alongside. While governments and legislation cannot always move fast enough to cope with these burgeoning issues and the ever-inventive minds of those exploiting the virtual environment, we can already see some degree of consistency in the international treatment of branding legal issues being achieved, not by governments but by the Internet community itself. This is particularly the case when one looks at the development of the ICANN UDRP. However, this means that brand owners will have to work with, as opposed to against, that community in encouraging good brand practices.

Governments have always been slow to deal together outside their own borders but brand owners in the virtual world must find ways to deal with the dichotomy between the territorial nature of current legal protection for brands and the lack of any national borders on the Net.

From the brand owners' perspective, the fundamental need to secure and enforce trade mark rights remains and, if anything, has assumed even greater significance. Indeed, the Internet has raised businesses' awareness of the importance of trade mark registrations and the territorial nature of trade mark rights.

For any legal adviser specializing in this area of law, it is now more important than ever to be aware of and advise clients on the international perspective of trade in what is becoming an increasingly small world.

robertherbold

Robert J. Herbold
Executive Vice President and
Chief Operating Officer
microsoftcorporation

Robert J. (Bob) Herbold is Executive Vice President and Chief Operating Officer of Microsoft Corporation, the leading worldwide provider of software for personal computers. He is responsible for worldwide operations at Microsoft, including finance, manufacturing and distribution, information systems, human resources, corporate services and corporate privacy and security. He also spends significant time representing Microsoft in press/community/industry situations. Herbold is a member of Microsoft's business leadership team, which shares responsibility with Bill Gates, Microsoft's Chairman, for broad strategic and business planning for the entire company. Prior to joining Microsoft in 1994, he was formerly Senior Vice President, Advertising and Information Services, at the Procter & Gamble Company where he was responsible for the company's worldwide advertising/brand management operations, as well as all marketing related services.

12 a look ahead: **e-biz in the new millennium**

If you look at what is happening in the world today with respect to services such as television, radio, newspapers and telephony, you see it all moving toward digital signals or bits, the same medium as online services and the Internet. Additionally, with software getting friendlier and easier to use, in the future you won't have to think about the notion of going out to the Internet; software will make all this content readily available and easy to use. You'll have all kinds of devices available that enable you to get at information easily. And what we used to call "going out to the Internet" will be irrelevant. That notion will disappear.

We will continue to see dramatic increases in the productivity of the microprocessor, due to continuing miniaturization. Also, we will continue to find new ways to pump more bits through the same piece of fiber optic wire. So, when we see all of these technologies continuing to increase in their capability, you just know that we are truly in for "digital convergence" of information and entertainment.

For example, you will have a wire or set of wires coming into your home. One of them may be brought to you by the company you used to call your cable company, one may be supplied by the organization you used to call the telephone company, but those wires will simply carry digital bits. And those bits will come flying into the home and go into a box that sorts them out, with some of the bits being associated with what we used to call telephone conversation, some of the bits going to a monitor in another room which looks like what we used to call television and some of the bits going to the den where children are doing their homework at a keyboard and monitor; something that looks very much like the thing we used to call the Internet. But, it will simply be a set of services such as news, weather, sports, reference material, shopping, movies and all sorts of entertainment and so forth in a portfolio of all these different kinds of capabilities. There will be a much better set of searching schemes to find key information. All of these services delivered via one wire in digital form is what we call digital convergence.

Today, the Internet is a bit rugged to use. When you do a search today, you get this long list of random associations to the word or phrase you've put in. That will be improved significantly. The world of five to ten years out will be really exciting from the standpoint of information available to people, and there will be blurring of the barriers, so to speak, of those lines of demarcation between what we used to call telephony and television and Internet experiences and email and things like that. This is the world into which we're heading.

In that world, all of a sudden, advertising becomes an important component for a variety of reasons. It represents the advertiser's dream, because it enables people to get advertising in the context of what it is that they're doing. If you're probing for information with regard to automobiles, where you are probing is a great place for an auto manufacturer to place advertising related to cars. These technologies will emerge as a great marketing tool to do a better job than ever before of isolating target audiences and delivering clear messages.

"Brands will play an important role online in the future, but the term 'online' will disappear and be replaced by digital information services."

Marketing is a very simple discipline. It has three basic rules. Number one, define, very concisely, the target audience for your product or service. Number two, define the message you want to deliver to that target audience and make it as brief and persuasive as possible. Number three, pick the media tool that carries that message concisely to that target audience without a whole lot of waste (that is, delivery to people not in your target audience).

Today, the marketing vehicles we have available to us are incredibly sloppy. For example, while some mass-audience-oriented consumer products can use television productively, it vastly overshoots most target audiences. With digital convergence, we should be able to do a much better job than ever before in getting around those kinds of problems. In fact, these new information services should be a marketer's dream. Given that, I'm a firm believer that most of these services brought to you via digital convergence will in fact be free in the future, for the same reason that the world of television and radio are free today – they are very valuable advertising tools!

"Digital convergence," as we are defining it, is just too good of a marketing device for that not to happen.

Now let's talk about devices. What we have called the personal computer business is now evolving literally into an explosion of different types of information appliances, with the low end being a simple cellular phone and the high end being powerful personal computers. The pocket PCs that are emerging today are quickly evolving to be a cellular phone and a device for sending email messages and a device for getting information off the Internet. All kinds of creative devices will emerge in the next few years, and they will all interact in some way or another with all those information services we've just talked about. I think that one of the goals of all the technology players is to make these devices simple enough to use so that ten years from now 75–80% of households will be taking advantage of some aspects of the full spectrum of digital convergence services.

What's important is that great software will enable those various services to take into account what kind of device the individual is using at that time, and appropriately format the services so that the information can be sent down to that device in a way that makes sense. The new software architecture that we're pursuing at Microsoft is precisely focused on that scenario, so when I send you a voice mail message, the system is smart enough to say, "Oh wait a minute, he's not on a telephone, he's on a personal computer. I'll send it as an email message and he can click on it and it will simply play on his PC." Or it might say, "Whoops, he's not on that personal computer at all, he's got his handheld device on, so I can send this thing as a true voice mail message in the traditional way." The system will be smart enough to adjust to that.

Microsoft is not an entertainment company or a content company. We're a software company and our job is to create great software, so that as those digital bits come flying into that household, we provide the capability (an operating system in a set top box) to sort them out into useful services.

Naturally, we want to be the operating system that helps to make the services happen with the greatest of ease. We also want to provide a lot of software capabilities that enable organizations to build great services. So we're kind of an infrastructure company. But we're also somewhat of a services company if you look at MSN.com, which on a world basis has more past-four-week-users than any other web location in the world. MSN.com is simply an accumulation of services, some from Microsoft, but mostly from others. In the future, people will want handy, easy to use services that provide (on a variety of devices) news, weather, sports and all the personal and work-related information that you need to get through the day. We'll be in that kind of business in the future as well. That is all about great software, which is our skill and how we hope to contribute to the future.

Brands will play an important role online, but the term online will disappear and be replaced by digital information services. I don't think the notion of an e-brand is any different from a brand itself. A brand mentally represents a set of services or attributes or capabilities that you've learned about through use and/or advertising. And brands will exist in the digital convergence world that we're discussing, just as they exist in the world today, and there will be some services that are only available electronically. I guess you could characterize eBay as an "e-brand" today, but I like to think of it more in the context of just a brand. You know the service it provides and its reputation, either through use, advertising or hearsay. When I think of Barnes & Noble, I think of the availability of books, whether online or physically. That is their brand identity. Clearly, the reputation of these brands, and any brand, will be determined by the services and capabilities that they offer to the consumer, and their advertising.

Successful branding in the future, no matter what industry we are talking about, will probably use a different profile of media tools to deliver their messages versus what they use today. Today, we're still at the point where television is the most broadly used media vehicle, radio is second, newspapers are third and online advertising just moved into number four position in regard to media dollars. We have to realize that it is the very early days for online advertising; it is just being born and it is one of the fastest growing media tools. For any marketing problem, it gets back to the basics of having a clear and motivating message for a product or service, knowing the target audience, and then finding the media tool that best isolates that target. Online capabilities include a lot of self-selections. For example, if I've gone to the Internet to a sports location, and I've probed down further into a fly fishing location where I'm hunting up information, there's a high probability that I'm a fly fisherman. Consequently, if you are marketing a fly rod for fly fisherman you have a great place to put your advertising. That kind of precise self-selection hasn't existed in the past. You've had to reach for "specialty" magazines, or something similar, as your advertising tool, and often they didn't exist for the target audience focus you wanted. Now, you have this incredibly targeted vehicle where the people have self-selected to get to the location to receive the advertising. That is euphoric from the perspective of branding and advertising!

These kinds of new targeting capabilities underscore the need for the marketer to determine a product's target audience very carefully. Just as an example, we have a game here at Microsoft called Age of Empires. It has a target audience of boys/young males between 12 and 25 years old. They account for a huge portion of the revenue. So, that is the target audience for that product. Consequently, we need to hunt for media vehicles that ideally deliver to that target audience and no other. So, is there a media vehicle that delivers to us that narrow "gamer" target audience via self-selection? There are, in fact, websites that cater to gamers, and, in the future, such gamer-focused "information services" will probably be far more mature than they are today.

Another robust example is the target audience of purchasers of luxury cars. Getting detailed information about automobiles is wildly popular on the Internet today, since people want to be armed with detailed cost and performance data before they go through the purchase exercise. So far, the

Internet has skewed a bit high in terms of income and education. Consequently, luxury car manufacturers have been very active in using the Internet for advertising, and appropriately so. It's a good decision on their part in regard to those three basics of marketing – the target audience, the message, and the media tool. These sites on the Internet that focus on information about automobiles are great media tools to deliver some incredibly good messages to the luxury car audience.

On the Internet, to some degree, you're enabling the consumers to define their own advertising experience. When a user of the Internet goes to an auto-focused website and goes to the luxury car section, the marketer of a luxury car ought to be willing to pay handsomely to put a message in front of that Internet user. So, to some extent, the user is defining their ad experiences based on the websites they visit.

Given such concise targeting, all of a sudden advertisers are willing to spend a lot more money per message, because the people who are being exposed to this advertising are very highly disposed to spend money in the category. This user self-selection gives us a tremendous new capability, bringing the user into these very precise target groups from which marketers can take notice and take advantage. This makes these new capabilities very exciting.

Advertisers might say that the downside of digital convergence is that there is less "forced viewing" of advertising and there are some categories that need forced viewing because these are categories of low interest. For example, you find very few people hunting for information about detergents. Consequently, online services don't add a lot in terms of marketing capabilities for that particular category of business. In fact, you can claim that low interest categories of business have been significantly advantaged in the past by forcing viewers to watch television advertising. Forced viewing of television advertising spots will continue to exist, but there will be less of that in the future. Forced viewing will continue to exist in live broadcasts (such as key sporting events, key news events, and so on). On the other hand, in a world of digital convergence, many advertising opportunities will be much more interactive and self-selecting which represent huge pluses to the marketers if their category is of moderate to high interest.

The lower interest categories can build their brands in other ways, including sponsoring live events and providing information directly to their users. Stepping back, every marketer has their own challenges and what these new capabilities will represent five or ten years from now is simply a new set of media tools, looking at it from a marketer's perspective.

Brand building and brand equity will continue to be incredibly important. Brand equity is a predisposed preference (or dislike!) for a brand based on your accumulated experience with the use of that product, as well as the advertising that portrays the product over time. You build up a mental bank account in regard to those products and build trust or skepticism levels. Clearly, brands need to keep themselves very current in regard to the product offerings and their image.

I think it's been fascinating to watch the rapid takeoff in the use of the Internet for financial equities trading. These services have become quite popular and it's interesting to notice that the one with the highest number of users is Schwab. Other established brokerage firms that haven't appeared on the Internet as quickly have ended up with a somewhat old-fashioned image. It's easier than ever for a trademark to go out of date, because the technologies are moving so fast that you can launch exciting new capabilities and services very quickly and very often. It's also much easier to create a valuable trademark very quickly in this kind of world. One example that I use is MSNBC, the news service. It's on the web, as well as on cable TV. That news service has become popular very quickly both on television, and the Internet. In fact, on the Internet, MSNBC is the number one news location. In three years, they've created the market leader while also greatly enhancing the overall trademark by having a very contemporary looking new 24-hours news channel on cable TV as well. The combination of those two things has caused a brand to emerge very, very quickly. Charles Schwab is also an example of a great job of getting in and providing capabilities in an online setting, but also managing their established business very well. Because of that, they've emerged with a very contemporary image.

The advertising agencies are reacting slowly to the Internet. One of the problems with human beings is that they get good at something and they want to keep doing that thing because they're good at it, and they don't recognize that the world has changed around them. We're all subject to that. In fact, Clayton Christiansen's book, *The Innovators' Dilemma* is all about this issue of human beings being trapped by their own success, and thus compromising their ability to really march out and be distinctive in the future and take advantage of important trends. Let's face it, people are good at patting themselves on the back with respect to their perceived skills at established things. We all have to watch out that we don't get that disease. In the case of an ad agency, that means creating marketing resources that can take advantage of new media devices in a very aggressive way. So ad agencies have to recraft their skills just like everybody else.

In the information technology industry, companies are very vulnerable. They have to stay on top of technology trends, or face big problems! In fact, any company in this industry is only 18–24 months away from big business problems if they don't consistently innovate. People in the information technology industry are much more aware of the fact that they better change or they are going to get run over. Change is a lot more of a given in the information technology industry compared to other industries, where you get people who don't have that attitude at all.

Brands such as Coca-Cola constantly worry about what it takes to keep that trademark fresh in people's minds and keep it contemporary. They have traditionally done that primarily through television advertising. They also must look at the new and quickly evolving world and say, "What are my media alternatives"? And ten years from now, the media alternatives will be dramatically different from today. They will have to put together a media plan that continues to support those image attributes that they want to associate with the Coca-Cola brand. There will be some television as we know it today and some televised events that are live as we discussed previously, and there will be a bunch of new media tools. And Coke will have to decide how they market their brand in a media world that has many options. It's a somewhat perplexing problem, because a brand that is primarily dependent on keeping its image contemporary, and doesn't have product characteristics or services that significantly improve regularly, has a very critical communications challenge. Coke has this huge audience and it will be interesting to see how they get their messages in front of people as mass audience television continues to shrink and fragment.

When you think about how the Internet and true digital convergence will change our habits and lifestyles in ten years, most experts believe there will be tons of information sources, e-shopping and an explosion of entertainment alternatives and it will all become a lot easier to get to. Does it eliminate "physical shopping"? No! Shopping centers will be alive and well because there's an important emotional component to going shopping (relax, people watch, unwind!), as well as the need to physically see, feel and experience things and often to just go "impulse shopping" when you don't know precisely what you want. Of course, there are times when I want to order a particular sweater just by taking my handheld device and pulling up a description of it and ordering it from that vendor that had the trademark or brand that I've trusted or used before. And there are times when I just want to relax and do something to blow off the steam … so, I go over to the shopping center to wander around, relax a bit, and do some people watching! I did a presentation to shopping center owners about two years ago and there were thousands of them in the audience. The thing that surprised them was the research I presented that showed that "just relaxing and wandering around stores" was very high on the list of reasons to go to a shopping center! If you know exactly what you want and know what you want to pay for it, online services may be better. But the important thing to realize is that the world is not going to go one way or the other. People want it both ways. And I think transactions will be very natural in both the electronic and traditional mode.

Privacy and security are emerging as very big issues. And there are great technology leads being pursued by companies such as Microsoft to provide individuals with tons of privacy and tons of security, and we as an industry need to get those capabilities into mainstream use. With regard to transactions, there are an increasing number of people using their credit cards online, and not having any security or privacy problems. On the other hand, we're not where we need to be in terms of the security and privacy issues as far as building up the confidence of the general public.

We will eventually get to a world that won't require paper money, coins or check writing. The smart card has the potential to achieve such a dream world. The "smart" capability may take the form of a credit card with a chip in it, or it may be a chip embedded in your cell phone and you just call an ATM or walk up to an ATM machine, infrared it, and it will electronically pass you your $200 withdrawal, or subtract an amount as you pay a bill. And when you go to that drink machine, you point that device at the drink machine, and out comes a Diet Coke and it has subtracted a dollar from your device. These devices will have an encryption code so that only you can power it up. That world is coming. There are devices today in drink machines in Japan and the drink suppliers can access them through radio waves and find out how many units still exist in the machines so that they can be replenished at the right time. That kind of stuff is going to be very exciting.

Television as we know it today will be replaced by a huge menu of catalogued content and the availability of key live programming. For example, I might want to watch game six of the famous 1975 World Series. I can order that, go to my big screen in my study and watch it. And two hours later, I might want to watch a live football game, then two hours later I want to look for a piece of information or some catalogued material relating to my favorite hobby. All of this will be easily available. Another big change that the Internet is bringing is incredible depth of information about current big news events. On MSNBC, the online news service, 24 hours before a hurricane hits the East Coast, the MSNBC weather service has nine or ten times the normal traffic. Why? Because you not only see what's going on with that hurricane, you get incredible, in-depth information. People who will be impacted by the storm, or who have loved ones that live in the path of the storm, want such information. You can see weather maps, all kinds of forecasts and video clips of the storm – a rich portfolio of information about this hurricane. Let's consider the alternatives for getting such information: you could wait for the six-o'clock news and see if they spend two minutes on the subject. You could buy today's newspaper with 6–12-hour-old information or you could listen to a radio news program. You could phone somebody who lives in the area. But the Internet gives you an incredible amount of rich, detailed information about this occurring event, so it's no wonder that the traffic multiplies by a factor of nine or ten at that time. When you step back and think about information entertainment and news, and the upcoming explosion of capabilities, you realize that we are really in for amazing times.

As with most subjects, as we move into the future, there will be a lot that will remain the same and there will be a lot that will change. The things that will remain the same are the basic fundamentals of marketing – isolating a target audience, knowing what message you want to deliver to a number of that target audience, and then selecting a media tool that enables you to deliver that message to that target. That will not change. Another thing that won't change is the role of brands and trademarks. They will potentially represent different things in your mind, but the notion of having brand attributes appear in your mind that are positive and negative, relative to that brand, will not change. What will change is the delivery mechanisms for information, entertainment, telephony, and so on, and the convenience with which you can get at these things. We will experience the convergence of a set of services that you used to think were separate – television, telephony, the Internet, newspapers, and so on. As these capabilities converge, there will be a major change in terms of how our products and services are marketed and delivered.